How To Play Guitar Modes

for beginners & intermediate students

By

Dwayne Jenkins

Introduction

When it comes to playing guitar solos and melody lines on the guitar, there is a lot of mystery. Especially when you mention guitar modes. This is the phrase that makes most guitar players scratch their heads and go "huh?"

The truth of the matter is that modes really aren't too difficult to learn and understand if you are taught correctly about them. This book will take out the confusion, and allow you to make sense of them.

<u>How To Play Guitar Modes</u> will show you in a very simple manner what they are all about. How they are just seven scales that are taken out of the seven notes of the major scale. See, you just learned something that makes them easier already.

In modern music we use a system of majors and minors. Either we have a major scale, or we have a minor scale. The seven modes can be broken down into these two categories. Depending on the notes within the individual scales.

We will learn more about this as the training progresses. Along with how to read notation, create guitar licks, mode scale formulas, chord voicings, arpeggios, and much, much more. All this will allow you to increase your understanding of how guitar modes work on the guitar.

The modes are latin and the word means "manner", or "method" and originated in ancient Greece. This gives them greek names. Names such as Phrygian, Lydian, Aeolian, etc. It is these names that make them seem a bit mysterious to the outsider.

With this simple-to-understand training, you will not be an outsider for long. You will easily see how they work within the major scale and how you can use them yourself to create guitar solos in any musical key you choose to do so.

As we progress learning about the major scale, why the notes are specific to each key and why the modes are specific to each note within the key, all the mystery will begin to make sense. Just take it one step at a time and you will develop an understanding of modes as they relate to the guitar.

So, if you're ready to dive in and see what all the fuss is about, how you can use modes to enhance your guitar playing, knowledge of the fretboard and music theory in general, then turn the page and let's get started.

Table of contents

Chapter 1 Getting Started

Lesson 1: What is a mode?

A mode is a selection of notes within the major scale of the key that it is taken out of. Starting on a particular note of the major scale. The major scale (any major scale) has seven notes and each one of these notes has a mode that is created off of it.

For example, if we look at the notes within the key of C major, the notes are:

C D E F G A B & C

Give each one of these notes a number value and we have:

C D E F G A B C
1 2 3 4 5 6 7 8

There will be a mode created from each one of these notes. Since the scale starts and ends with the same note, we only count it once. That means the scale has 7 notes. Technically, C-B. The last C will be the start of the scale in the next octave.

This is what we will be learning in this book. These 7 modes and how we can use them in our guitar playing.

Lesson 2: Is it the same as a scale?

Well, yes and no. Let me explain. All modes are scales, but not all scales are modes. There are literally thousands of scales that can be played on the guitar. This goes for chords as well. Crazy huh? The reason for this is because of the notes that make up these scales and chords.

So technically modes are scales because they are made up of a selection of notes within certain keys. But they only come from the notes of a major key. Not a minor key. This is what makes them so mysterious.

A scale is technically defined as a selection of ascending and descending notes within certain intervals (distance between them) that can be used to form melodies and guitar solos. These can be both major scales such as in G major, as well as in minor, such as in E minor.

When it comes to minor scales there are many. Natural minor, harmonic minor, melodic minor, etc. But with the modes, there are only the 7 modes because of the fact that they come specifically from the 7 notes that reside in the major scale. If there were 10 notes, there'd be 10 modes.

This is what makes them different from scales. Are they a selection of notes like a scale? Yes. Do they have all kinds of different variations like scales? No. See what I mean by yes and no?

Once you get down the fundamentals of why there are only 7 modes and where they come from, they become easier to understand and work with. This is what we are shooting for in this book.

Lesson 3: Why learn to use them?

Learning about the modes and how to use them will help you to increase your understanding of many great things.

It will help you to learn and understand:

1. Notes within the major scale
2. Chords that can be created within the major scale
3. Guitar licks that can be created for solos
4. Ear training by learning note intervals
5. How to build finger strength & dexterity
6. Learn & write songs easier
7. How the music notes works better in theory

And much, much, more. All these things will help you to increase not only your guitar playing but your whole overall musicianship. And that is what you are shooting for by learning this information.

This is the true benefit over just playing guitar by ear. You get to fully understand what it is you are playing.

There is nothing wrong with playing by ear. It is a skill I recommend you learn and later in this training I will go over some things you can do to help develop this. But if you are going to study diagrams, notes and theory, you want to develop an understanding of why it all works the way it does.

4

Lesson 4: Reading tablature

The best way to fully understand modes is to be able to not just play them but to read them as well. Remember, music is a language and you want to learn how to read it, write it, and speak it. Playing modes on the guitar is the speaking part of it. The other part is the reading and writing.

This is where tablature (tabs for short) and diagrams come in. Here in lesson 4 we are going to look at how to read tablature for quick reference of these 7 modes. This will help you to understand them better and be able to find them quicker along the fretboard.

Tablature has been around for many years and is a simple method of reading sheet music. It takes out the guesswork and is specifically designed for our purpose. We will be working with horizontal lines that represent the strings, and numbers that represent the frets.

Here is an example of tablature. The 6 horizontal lines represent your guitar strings with your biggest string (your sixth string) being on the bottom.

The reason for this is because in sheet music of any kind, the lowest note will always be on the bottom. So when reading tabs, you want to make sure to remember this. It is what makes this hard to read and understand for most people who play guitar.

That is why they choose to just play by ear.

Numbers represent the frets that you will be playing on. So in the example of tabs, there will be numbers on the lines.

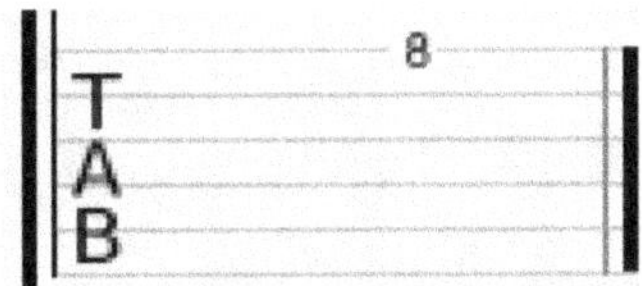

Here we have an example of a note at the eighth fret on the first string. This would be your smallest string.

Just think of the lines as being upside down from your guitar. I know, it is a bit confusing, but trust me, as you work with it, it'll get easier to understand and execute. Sorry, I didn't design it, I just teach it.

Here are some more examples:

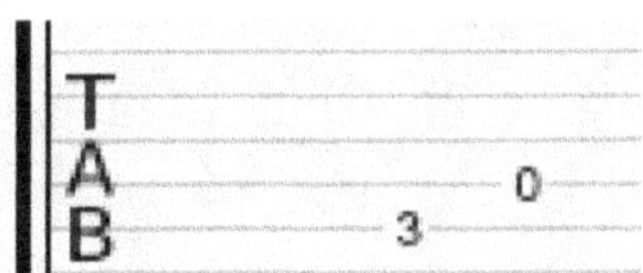

Here we have two notes that will be played one after the other. This example also shows an open note which is represented by a 0. This is when you play a string without putting a finger down on a fret. Here it will be on the 4th string from the top of your guitar. The open D string.

Here we have 4 notes played one after the other on the 6th and 5th strings. This is part of the G major scale. Play it and you will hear the Do Re Mi Fa.

6

This is the basic fundamentals of how you read tablature. Lines and numbers. You just got to remember a couple of things:

1. Lines represent the guitar strings upside down
2. Numbers represent the frets that you play on

Now tabs don't show you everything like what fingers to use and timing sequence, but what they do is give you a simple basic place to start learning from. This is where they will benefit you in this musical training.

As we progress with other concepts like guitar licks, I will show you how to read those in tab at that time.   This will keep things simple and you will not be overwhelmed with too much information at one time. This is a very common frustration in learning music.

Lesson 5: Reading diagrams

Box pattern diagrams are another way of reading modes and scales. They are the same thing as tabs except instead of using numbers they use dots. Where you are located on the fretboard will be indicated by a number, but everything else will be dots.

Here's an example of what I mean:

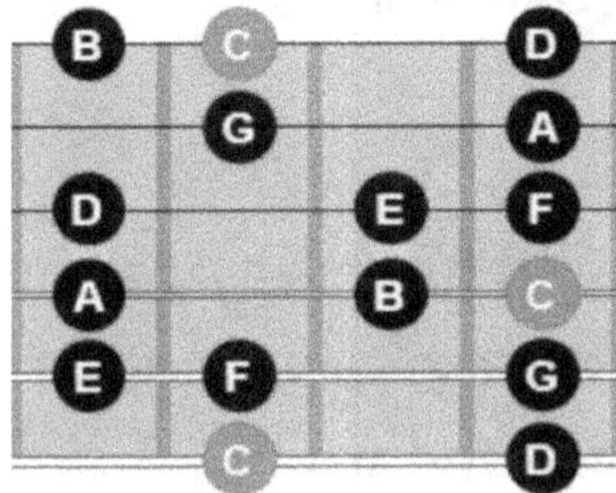

Here we have a box pattern diagram. Still have 6 horizontal lines that represent the strings and dots that represent where you place your fingers. In this particular example, the dots show what notes are being played in this mode.

Box pattern diagrams are a very common way to read modes and scales. The reason why they're called box pattern diagrams is because the notes line up in a box pattern shape. This makes them easier to learn and play when you use them.

Tablature and box pattern diagrams are the most common way to read modes and scales. For this training we will be looking at a bit of both. Mainly written tablature because I feel it is more beneficial to learn in the long run.

8

Chapter 1 Summary

In this introductory chapter we have looked at some basic fundamental principles that are very beneficial to learning and understanding modes.

First, we looked at what a mode is. A mode is a selection of notes that are derived from each of the notes that make up the major scale. There are 7 notes to the major scale so that means that there are 7 modes.

Second, we learned that a mode is similar to a scale but not exactly one. The difference is that with scales, there are many to choose from both major and minor, but with th modes there are only 7.

Third, we looked at why it was beneficial to learn them, and how they can benefit our playing. This will also allow us to communicate the language of music better and help us to unlock the mysterious guitar fretboard.

Fourth, we looked at how to read tablature or tabs for short. This is a very important lesson and I highly recommend you don't overlook it. Learning to read the written word can have huge benefits that you can add to your ability to play by ear.

Fifth, we looked at box pattern diagrams. Another common way of reading modes. A bit different from tabs, but similar. I also recommend you get familiar with this as well.

This first chapter will set the foundation for what's to follow. Make sure you fully understand these first few lessons as these lessons are designed to build upon each other as time goes on. This will make them easier to learn and quicker to understand.

Chapter 2 The Major Scale

Lesson 6: The C major scale

The easiest scale to begin learning is the C major scale. The reason for this is that it has no accidentals. Sharps or flats. The reason for this is because every major scale in the whole musical spectrum must conform to the Do Re Mi that we are so familiar with.

If it doesn't conform to the Do Re Mi, then it isn't a major scale. Make sure you remember this. The notes of each major scale must conform to certain intervals to make this happen. An interval is the distance between two notes.

Here is the C major scale:

```
C   D   E   F  G  A   B  C
1   2   3   4  5  6   7  8
Do  Re  Mi  Fa So La  Ti Do
```

As you can see it is made up of 8 notes. If we give each note a number value, C is 1, D is 2, E is 3, and so on. We can also see that each note represents the Do Re Mi. All major scales will have this. The notes will change, but they will all have a number value and a syllabus.

The seven modes in this key, will come out of these 7 notes of the C major scale.

Since we now know what the seven notes are in this key, we can now look at the seven modes. These are:

1. C Ionian
2. D Dorian
3. E Phrygian
4. F Lydian
5. G Mixolydian
6. A Aeolian
7. B Locrian

Seven notes equal 7 modes. Each mode will start on one of these notes that are in the C major scale. So for instance, if you wanted to play the Ionian mode in the key of C major you would start on the C note. But if you wanted to play the Lydian mode you'd start on the F note of the scale.

Does this make sense?

If we go through the C major scale along the fretboard on the 5th string, the notes would be on these frets:

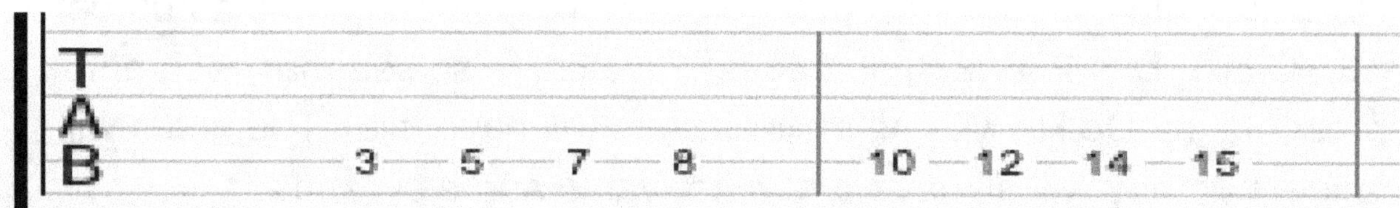

If you play these notes along your fretboard all on the 5th string, you'll see they have the Do Re Mi sound. This is the C major scale played along the fretboard.

Here is another example of the C major scale played on the 6th string:

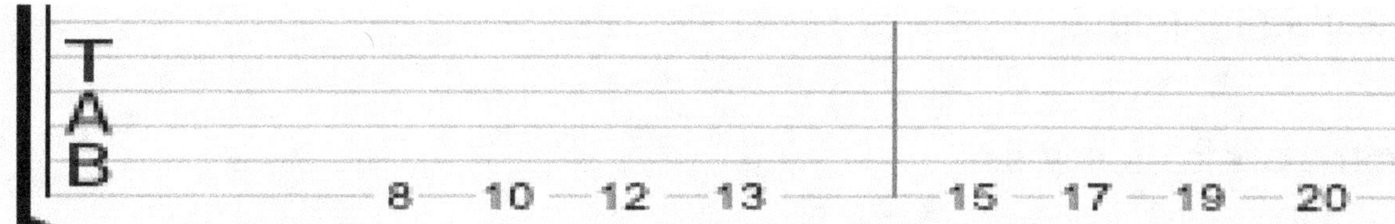

As you can clearly see, the notes are the same, just on a different string and on different frets. But the Do Re Mi still applies. This will be the same anywhere you play this scale on the guitar.

It is important to know these frets and what notes they are because this is where you will play the 7 modes. For example, If you were to play the Ionian mode in the key of C it would start on the 8th fret. Because that is a C note.

On the other hand, if you were to play the Phrygian mode in the key of C, it would be played at the 12th fret because that is an E note. And if you notice on page 10, the Phrygian is the third mode and starts on the third note of the scale. In the key of C major, that would be the E note.

Of course it would be a different note for each key, but the Phrygian mode will always be the third mode in any major key. It's just the note that will change. You'll see what I mean as we get to other keys.

Now that we know the seven mode names and where they would be played along the fretboard in the key of C major, let's look at them in more detail.

In the key of C major (actually any major key) you can make certain chords out of the notes within the key. This is important to know because the modes will relate to these chords.

The Chords are as follows:

1. C major
2. D minor
3. E minor
4. F major
5. G major
6. A minor (this is the natural minor)
7. B diminished

Like I said before, this is the same for all major keys. The 1, 4, & 5 will be major, the 2, 3, & 6 will be minor and the 7th will be diminished. The reason for this is because the 7th becomes the leading note in the major scale. This gives it a different feel and character.

This is important to know because the 7 modes will relate to this information.

Here are the 7 modes in the key of C major:

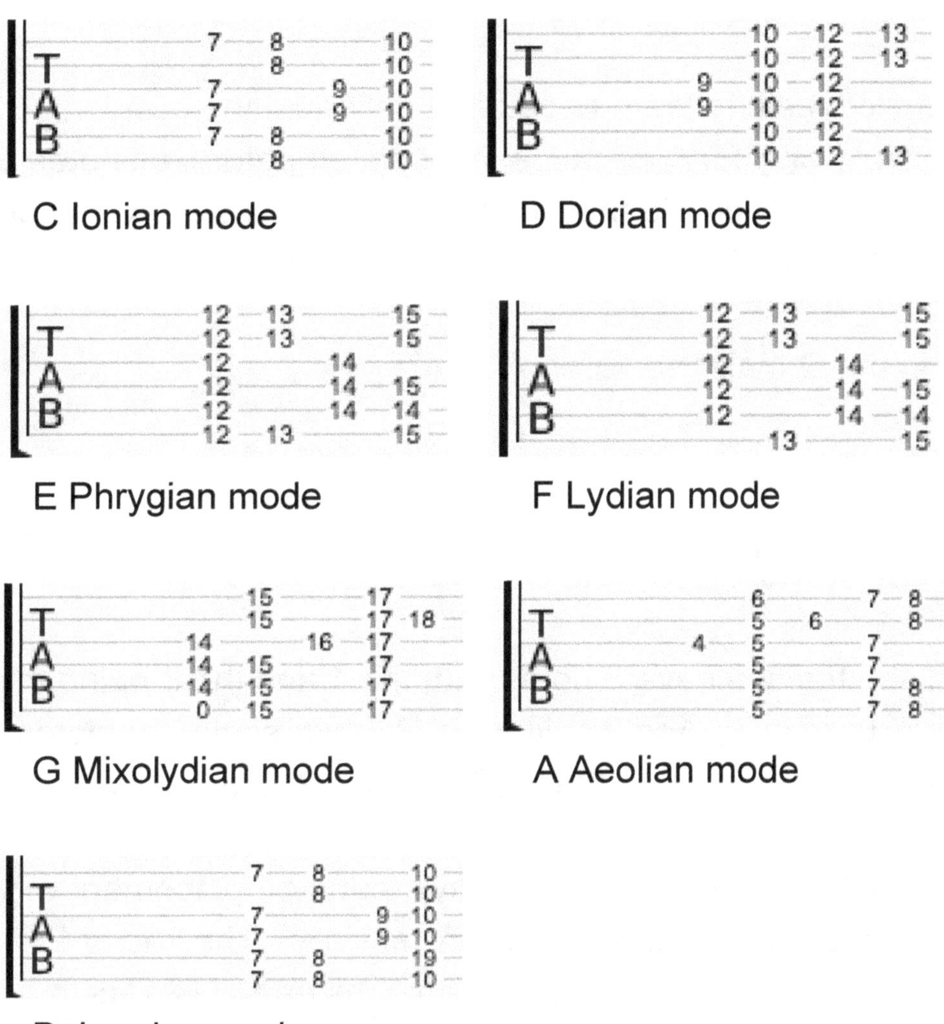

C Ionian mode

D Dorian mode

E Phrygian mode

F Lydian mode

G Mixolydian mode

A Aeolian mode

B Locrian mode

Notice how the Phrygian mode is exactly the same as the Lydian mode except for one note difference, and the Locrian mode is the same as the Ionian mode except for one note difference. This is because the 3 & 4 and the 7 & 8 are right next to each other in the scale.

I will explain this in fuller detail later in the training.

Lesson 7: The G major scale

This is the second major scale to learn because it only has one accidental. That note is the F#. Why only F#? Because like I stated before, all notes must be diatonically correct to create the Do Re Mi. In the case of G major, all notes will be natural except the F#.

Here are the notes in the G major scale:

```
G   A   B   C   D   E   F#  G
1   2   3   4   5   6   7   8
Do  Re  Mi  Fa  So  La  Ti  Do
```

Once again we can see that we have 8 notes with the 1 and the 8 being the same. So that leaves us with 7. And just like the C major scale, the notes relate to the numbers that are given to them. G is1, A is 2, B is 3, etc.

Now the modes will still be 7 as before and always, but their placement will be different because we are now playing in a different key. The key of G major. Now the Ionian mode will start on the G note instead of C. The Lydian mode will now start on C instead of F.

When we go through the notes in the scale and hear the Do Re Mi, it will be obvious why the F is sharpened and why the other notes are not. If we were to use a natural F in this key, it would not sound diatonically correct. So it must be sharpened.

Now that we know the seven notes, let's look at the seven modes:

1. G Ionian
2. A Dorian
3. B Phrygian
4. C Lydian
5. D Mixolydian
6. E Aeolian
7. F# Locrian

Here is the G major scale along the guitar fretboard:

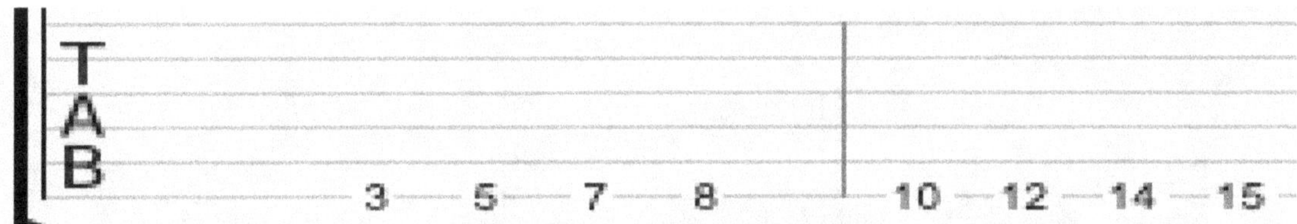

If you play these notes, you will hear the Do Re Mi in them. And if you know your notes along the fretboard, you'll see that they make up the notes I have described above. With the 7th note being an F#.

The location of these notes is vitally important because it tells you where you are going to play the modes in this key. Since the 3rd fret is a G note, this is where you'd play the Ionian mode. But if you were to play the D Aeolian mode, it would be played at the 10th fret.

The reason why this is so important to know is because this is what allows you to stay in key when you play. Which is the most common problem guitar players have when playing solos. Staying in key. If you know what to play and where to play it, you'll stay in key and sound good every time.

Here are the 7 modes in the key of G:

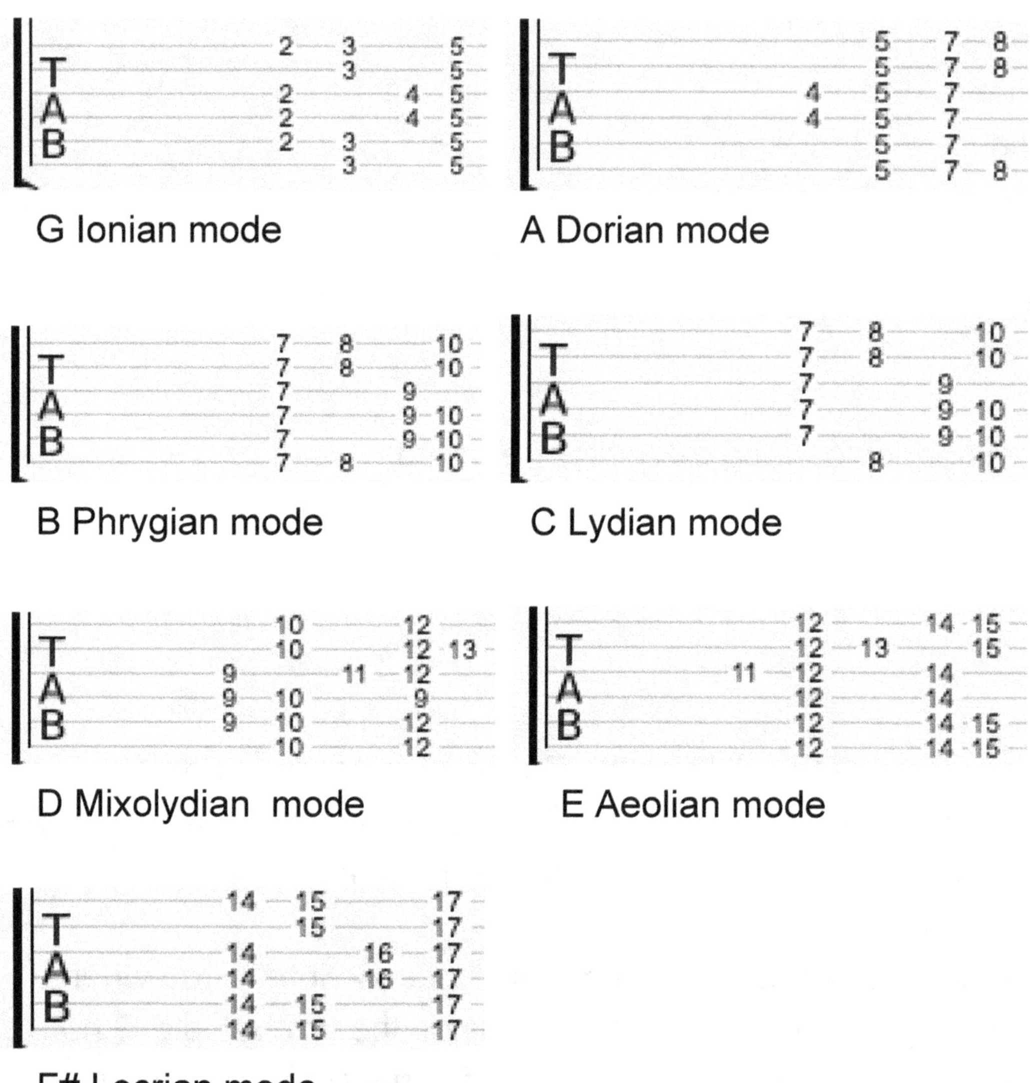

G Ionian mode

A Dorian mode

B Phrygian mode

C Lydian mode

D Mixolydian mode

E Aeolian mode

F# Locrian mode

After you play the locrian mode, you're right back to the Ionian mode at the 15th fret. As you can see, these are the same as in the key of C, they're just located in a different position.

These notes also represent chords just like we learned in the key of C. They're just in the key of G. Like G major, A minor, etc.

Lesson 8: The D major scale

The third scale to learn is the D major scale and the reason for this is that the D major scale has two accidentals. The F# and the C#. As before, this is so the notes line up correctly to create the Do Re Mi. This will be for all major scales and that is why the notes in each scale change.

Here are the notes in the D major scale:

D E F# G A B C# D
1 2 3 4 5 6 7 8
Do Re Mi Fa So La Ti Do

These eight notes are very important to memorize because they will represent where the modes will be located in this key. So for instance, the Ionian will be the D, the Dorian will be the E and so forth. If you want to play the Lydian mode in the key of D, it would be at the G position. G Lydian in the key of D.

Here are the notes in D major along the fretboard:

The D note on the 6th string is located at the 10th fret. To make this scale easier to learn the modes in, I put the last three notes in the first octave at the 7th, 9th, & 10th frets. Same notes, just in a different position. This will make executing the modes in this key easier.

Here are the 7 modes in the key of D major:

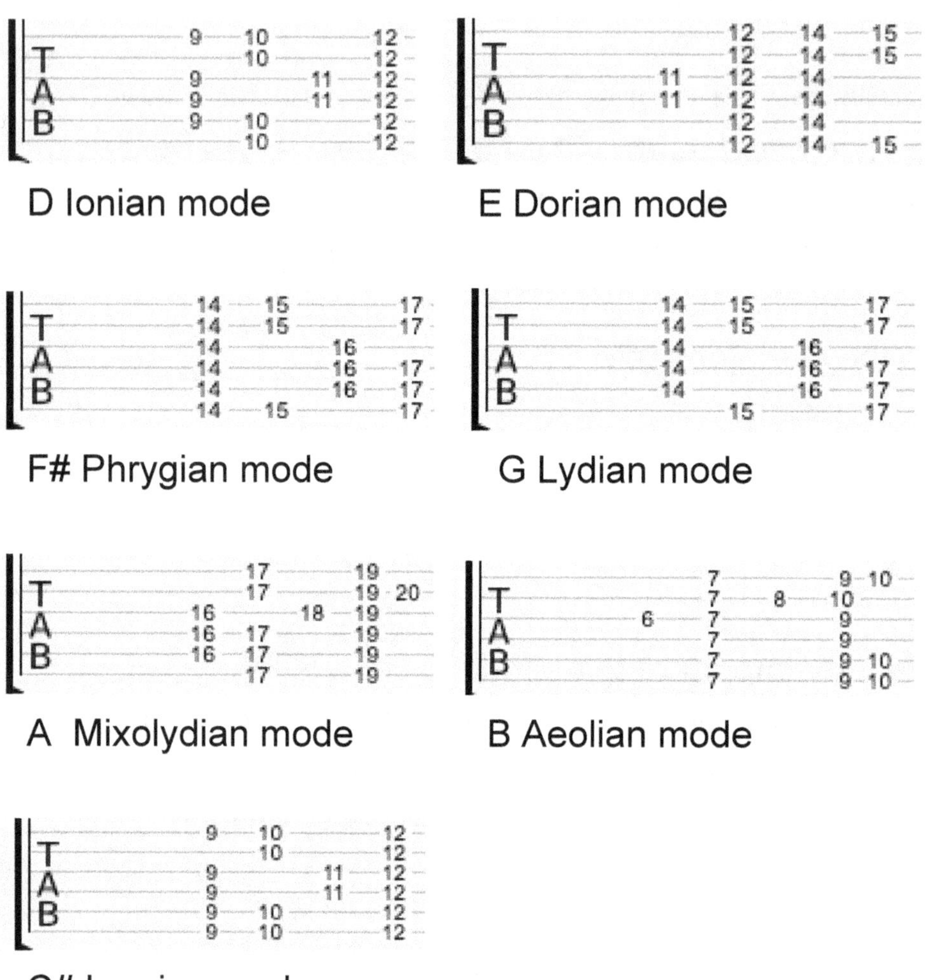

D Ionian mode

E Dorian mode

F# Phrygian mode

G Lydian mode

A Mixolydian mode

B Aeolian mode

C# Locrian mode

In the last two modes I placed them before the D note at the 10th fret on the 6th string because they are easier to play there. Notice also as before, the Phrygian & Lydian are the same, just one note difference. As well as the Ionian and Locrian mode. This is because of the ½ step difference.

Lesson 9: The A major scale

We choose the A major scale next because it has three sharps. I have chosen these keys to start with because they are most common and they build upon themselves with the accidentals. C has none, G has 1, D has 2, and A has 3.

Here are the note in the key of A major:

```
A   B   C#  D   E   F#  G#  A
1   2   3   4   5   6   7   8
Do  Re  Mi  Fa  So  La  Ti  Do
```

In future lessons, I'll explain how to find these notes very easily and be able to identify them in any key.

Notes of the A major scale along the fretboard are:

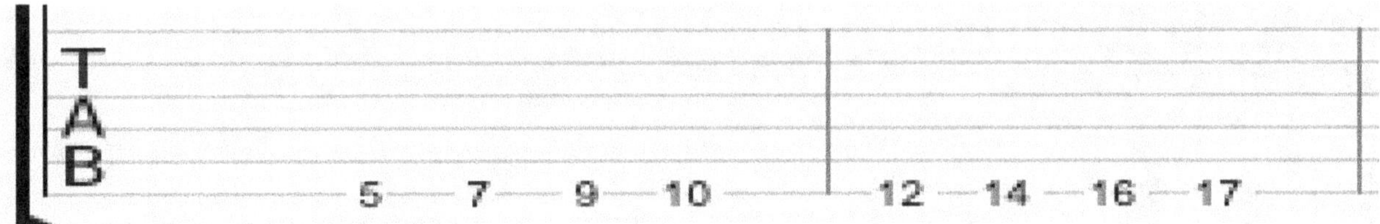

If you play these notes in this order along the fretboard, you will hear the familiar Do Re Mi. This is what you want to master with all your major scales. This will allow you to know exactly where to play the modes within any major key.

Here are the 7 modes in the key of A major:

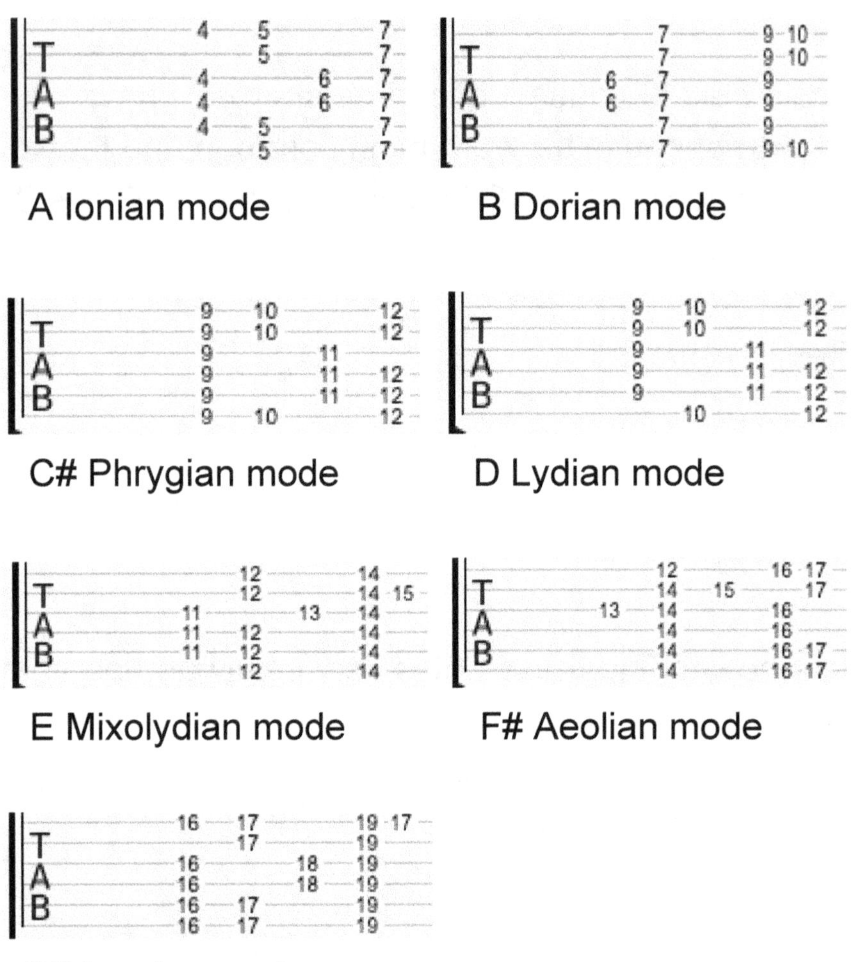

A Ionian mode

B Dorian mode

C# Phrygian mode

D Lydian mode

E Mixolydian mode

F# Aeolian mode

G# Locrian mode

As you can see, same as the other keys, the modes start on the individual notes of the scale. So if you want to play the Aeolian mode in the key of A major, you'd play it on the F# note. The Phrygian mode would be played on the third note C#, and the Mixolydian mode would start at the E.

Lesson 10: The E major scale

The E major scale is the one we choose next because it has four sharps in it. Once again, this is so the notes line up correctly to create the Do Re Mi that is necessary with all major scales. In the case of the E major scale, all notes will be natural except four.

Here are the notes in the E major scale:

```
E   F#  G#  A   B   C#  D#  E
1   2   3   4   5   6   7   8
Do  Re  Mi  Fa  So  La  Ti  Do
```

As we can see from the notes above, the 4 sharps in this key are the F#, G#, C#, and D#. This is very important to know because when we look at the modes for this key, some of them will start on these notes. Can you guess which modes they will be? What mode start on the C#?

Notes of the E major scale along the fretboard are:

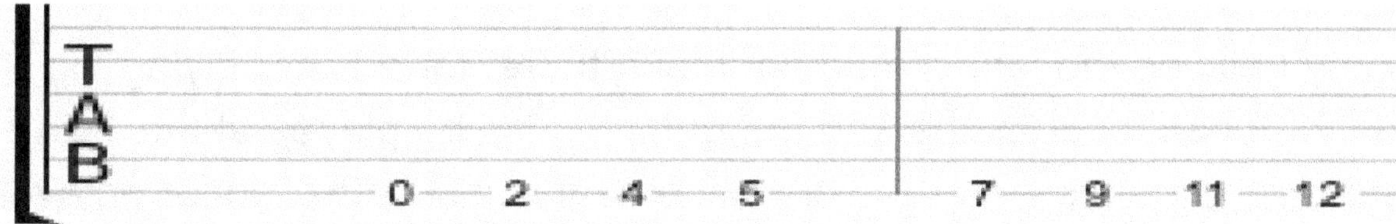

Since the E scale on the sixth string starts with the open E note, we'll play the Ionian mode at the 12th fret because it will be easier. We also will have the opportunity to play some of the other modes further up the neck as well when we get past the 12th fret.

Here are the modes in the key of E major:

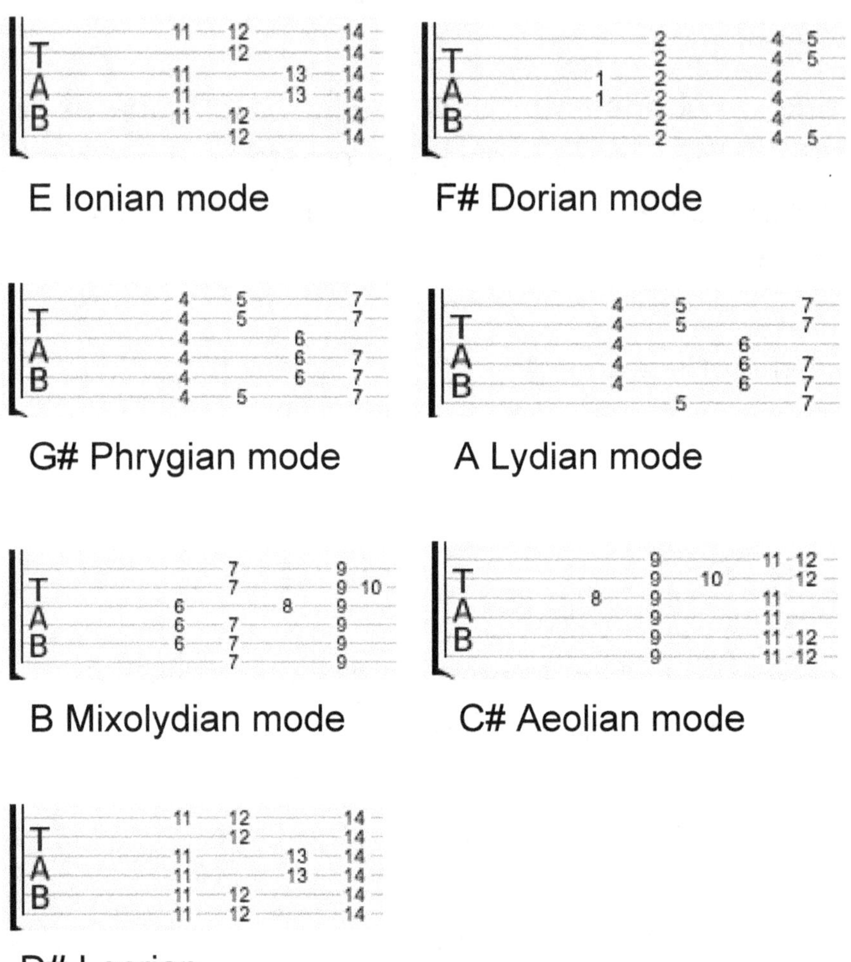

E Ionian mode   F# Dorian mode

G# Phrygian mode   A Lydian mode

B Mixolydian mode   C# Aeolian mode

D# Locrian

In this key I placed the Ionian mode at the 12th fret for easier playing. I placed the dorian mode at the 2nd fret but can also be played at the 14th fret as they are the same note. This placement is just in the higher octave. This key allows you to experiment.

Make sure you fully understand these modes and where they're located in this key. That way the next time someone says they have a song in the key of E, you'll know where to play.

Chapter 2 Summary

In this chapter we have covered the modes in 5 different keys. I chose these keys because they are most common. What is great about knowing them is that the information can be applied to all 12 keys in the musical spectrum.

First the key of C major. This key comes first because all notes are natural. No accidentals (sharps or flats) that is why it is chosen first in all music training.

Second comes the key of G major. This key has only one accidental. All other notes are natural. Not too hard to learn and a very common key in songs.

Third is the key of D. This key has two sharps. The F# that the key of G has but adds the C# as well. Plus it is located higher up the fretboard for a completely different sound then G.

Fourth is the key of A. This key has the F# & C# but adds one more, the G#. Plus this key resides in about the middle of the fretboard and this is what makes it very easy and common to play in.

Fifth is the key of E. This key has all three accidentals that the other four keys have and adds one more. The D#. This is the lowest note in standard tuning and therefore a very common key to play in as well.

The 7 mode shapes are the same in each key. It just a matter of where they are played that makes the difference. The Dorian mode will be the same shape in any key. It's just a matter of where it is played. If at the 10th fret, what key is it in?

Chapter 3 Seven Mode Chords

Lesson 11: Ionian mode (major)

Although the modes all come from the major scale, each mode represents a chord as well. Meaning that a certain type of chord resides within each mode. The Ionian mode is a major mode because the notes line up in such a way that a major chord can be played within it.

Let's look at this in more detail.

The notes of the C major scale are:

```
C  D  E  F  G  A  B  C
1  2  3  4  5  6  7  8
```

The C major chord formula is a 1 3 5. This means that we would choose the notes that relate to these numbers. As you can see, these numbers are in this mode. The C, E, & G. So we can come to the conclusion that this is a major mode.

If we wanted to make a C minor chord, we'd have to flatten the 3rd note. The E would become an E flat (Eb) and we can see that the notes in the Ionian mode do not conform to that.

Plus, when we play this mode in any key, it gives us the familiar Do Re Mi which is the major scale. So, by looking at the notes and listening to them as we play them, we can see that the Ionian mode is a major mode.

This goes for any key we choose to play them in. Let's look at a few more examples:

Ionian mode in the key of G major:

G A B C D E F# G
1 2 3 4 5 6 7 8

G major chord formula: 1 3 5. Notes within the mode are, G, B, & D. If we want to play G minor we need to flatten the 3rd note. We can see then that the B would need to become B flat. That is not in the mode.

Ionian mode in the key of D major:

D E F# G A B C# D
1 2 3 4 5 6 7 8

D major chord formula: 1 3 5. Notes within the mode are D, F#, & A. If we want to play D minor, same as before. Notes don't line up in the mode.

Ionian mode in the key of A major:

A B C# D E F# G# A
1 2 3 4 5 6 7 8

A major chord formula: 1 3 5. Notes within the mode are A, C#, & E. To play an A minor chord we need to do as before. Flatten the 3rd note to a C. This note does not reside within this mode.

This works with all keys the Ionian mode is played in.

Lesson 12: Dorian mode (minor)

This mode is considered a minor mode for the same reason the Ionian is considered a major. It is because of the way the notes line up.

Dorian mode in the key of C major:

D E F G A B C D
1 2 b3 4 5 6 b7 8

Here we start on the second note of the scale, the D note. As you can see, if we wanted to make a D major chord, we couldn't because the 3rd note of D (F#) is now flat. We could, however, make a D minor chord. The formula for a D minor chord is 1 b3 5. That would be the D, F, & A.

This works because these notes are in the Dorian mode. This lets us know that the Dorian mode is a minor mode. It is the flat third and flat seventh notes that give it its character and makes it sound different from the Ionian mode. Let's look at some more examples.

Dorian mode in the key of G major:

A B C D E F G A
1 2 b3 4 5 6 b7 8

Once again we start on the second note of G major, the A note. Can we make an A major chord? No, because the 3rd is now flattened to a natural C. But we can create an A minor chord. 1 b3 5. The A, C, & E.

As you can see, the Dorian mode is a minor mode because of the fact that you can create a minor chord but not a major unless you alter the notes. This is very important to remember, because each mode works well with certain chords and not others.

The reason for this is because of the way the notes are structured in each mode. Since the Ionian mode is a major mode, it will work best with major chords. D major, E maj7, A maj9, etc.

The Dorian mode, because of the way the notes in up in this mode will work better with minor chords. D minor, E minor 7, Bm7, etc. This is where knowing your notes comes in very handy.

By starting on a different note in the scale but still using the same notes of the scale, you create a different mood. This is what makes the modes so popular. They all have their own mood.

Three are major, three are minor and one is diminished (I will explain this later in this training) and it is this difference that sets their moods.

Once you learn the mode inside and out, you'll see what I mean when you play a barre chord in its position. When playing a major barre chord, the middle finger on the third string represents the third of the chord. Lift it off and you have a minor chord.

If you play a barre chord in the Dorian position, you will see very clearly that the way the notes line up, it is a minor barre chord you will need to play. The way the notes line up within the mode will dictate this.

Lesson 13: Phrygian mode (minor)

The third mode that we learned is the Phrygian mode. This is another minor mode because of the way the notes line up and how a minor chord fits within it.

Once again, if you play a minor barre chord in this mode no matter what key you're in, you'll see that the notes line up perfectly. But there is no note placement on the third string for the middle finger to form a major barre chord. That is why this is considered a minor mode.

Phrygian mode in the key of C major:

```
E  F  G  A  B  C  D  E
1 b2 b3 4  5 b6 b7 8
```

Here we start on the third note of the C major scale the E note. Starting here we can see that we create a flat 2, 3, 6, & 7. If we were to try to make a E major chord (1 3 5) we would need the notes E, G#, & B. But since the notes don't line up that way, we can't unless we alter the mode.

What we can do is make a E minor chord. Because we have a flat three in the mode. The G note. An E minor chord (1 b3 5) can be created with the notes E, G, & B. We could also create a Em7 chord (1 b3 5 b7) because those notes are present as well.

Does this make sense?

If you play this mode over these chords, you'll see that they sound really good together. Why? Because all the notes of the chords can be found in this mode. Let's look at another key.

Phrygian mode in the key of G major:

B C D E F# G A B
1 b2 b3 4 5 b6 b7 8

Once again, we can see that to create the B major 1 3 5, we would need the notes B, D#, & F#. But since the 3rd note is flattened we can't unless we alter the mode. But like before, we, we can create a B minor chord with the notes B, D, & F#.

Also like with the E Phrygian mode in the key of C, we can create a Bm7 chord as well. 1 b3 5 b7. Or a Bmb6 chord. 1 b3 5 b6. Can you see how this works and how this mode would work well with these chords?

All modes will work well with the chords that can be created out of them. Since each mode starts on a different note in the major scale, different chords can be created out of them.

It is just a matter of knowing your notes in the key that the modes are being created from and knowing chord formulas. The notes that create guitar chords. Majors, minors, etc.

Like for instance, a sus chord is where you move the 3 to the 4, or the 3 to the 2. So instead of the triad being a 1 3 5, it is now a 1 4 5 (sus 4 chord) or a 1 2 5 (sus 2 chord) and these can be created as well.

Lesson 14: Lydian mode (major)

In the Lydian mode, we find that this mode is a major just like the Ionian. Why? You should know this by now. Because of the way the notes line up. Let's take a look in further detail. In the key of C major the Lydian mode starts on the fourth note the F.

Lydian mode in the key of C major:

F G A B C D E F
1 2 3 #4 5 6 7 8

Here we can clearly see that we have a natural third in this mode. So with that being the case, we can create an F major chord with the notes F, A, & C. We couldn't however create the minor chords that we could create with the Phrygian mode because the note sequence doesn't allow for that.

This is how we determine that this is a major mode and not a minor like the Dorian and Phrygian. Let's look at this in another key.

Lydian mode in the key of G major:

C D E F# G A B C
1 2 3 #4 5 6 7 8

In the key of G major the F# is the 7th note, but in the key of C major it becomes a sharp fourth. We can also see that a C major chord with the notes C, E, & G can be created. As well as a CM7 (1 3 5 7) chord with the notes C, E, G, & B.

So with all this being said, we can conclude that the Lydian mode (the fourth mode) is a major mode. We now have discovered two major modes, the Ionian & Lydian, and two minor modes, the Dorian and Phrygian.

We have also discovered certain chords that can be created out of these modes and learned why they are relative. Why? Because they all come out of the mode and since that's the case, will work well played with that particular mode. Let's look at another key.

Lydian mode in the key of A major:

D E F# G# A B C# D
1 2 3 #4 5 6 7 8

If we start on the D note and play through the scale, we can see that the fourth note G is sharpened just like in the key of C. In the key of D, the G note would be natural and is now sharpened to create the #4 that is in the Lydian mode.

We can now come to the conclusion that the Lydian mode has a sharp fourth in it. And it is this fourth note that gives the mode its character and mood. Let's look at one more key.

Lydian mode in the key of D major

G A B C# D E F# G
1 2 3 #4 5 6 7 8

Once again, we can see that the 4th note is sharpened. In the key of G we would normally have a natural C, but in the lydian mode it is a C# just like in the other keys that we looked at.

Lesson 15: Mixolydian mode (major)

We now come to the Mixolydian mode. This is the mode played off of the 5th note in the scale. Let's look again at the key of C.

```
G A B C D E F G
1 2 3 4 5 6 b7 8
```

Here we can clearly see that this mode has a flat 7 in it. In the key of G major, the 7th note is a F#, but here in the Mixolydian mode it is flattened to fit into the notes of the major scale it comes out of which in this example is the key of C major.

We can also see that since the 3rd is natural and not flattened, we can make a G major chord (G, B, & D) as well as a Gsus4 chord (1 4 5) and also a G7 chord (1 3 5 b7) out of the Mixolydian mode.

The mixolydian mode would work well with any of these chords because the notes come right out of the mode as with all the other modes we have learned so far. Let's look at another key.

Mixolydian mode in the key of G major:

```
D E F# G A B C D
1 2 3  4 5 6 b7 8
```

Once again, we have the notes of the D major scale with a flat 7 in there. Normally in the key of D major, the C would be a C#, but to conform with the key of G major that the Mixolydian mode comes out of, it has to be flattened.

It is very important to remember why these modes are considered major and minor even though they all come out of the major scale. It is because of the way the notes lineup and the chords that can be created out of these note sequences.

If you need to learn more about chord theory, I recommend you check out my book <u>Rhythm Guitar Alchemy.</u> This book explains chord theory and how it can help you to improve your rhythm playing.

Mixolydian mode in the key of E major:

B C# D# E F# G# A B
1 2   3   4 5   6   b7 8

In the key of B major, we have 5 sharps C#, D#, F#, G#, & A#. In the Mixolydian mode we have a flattened 7th and in this case it would be the A note flattened from A# to natural A. This way it will conform to the notes in the key of E major.

It will also give the characteristics of the key of B major with a flat 7th in it. This will give the key a different tone and mood when played over chords in a chord progression.

What chords can be played out of the Mixolydian mode?

Major, Sus2, Sus4. Maj6, Dom7 (chord with a b7 in it) and all these chords will work well with the Mixolydian mode because the notes all come out of it in any key you choose to play it in.

Chapter 3 summary

In this chapter we have looked at 5 of the modes individually and discovered that so far three are major and two are minor. The reason for this is because of the way the notes line up.

Ionian mode. This is your natural major mode. It follows the Do Re Mi that we are so familiar with. In this mode we have a natural third note and this is what's needed to make major chords. Chords like C major, C maj6, C maj7, etc.

Dorian mode. Starts off the 2nd note of the major scale and the notes line up in such a way that it creates a flattened third and flattened 7th note. This is how we can conclude it is a minor mode. Minor chords can be created. Minor, m7th, m6th, etc.

Phrygian mode. Starts on the third note of the scale and is also a minor mode because it has a flat 2, 3, 6, & 7 in it. It is these flats within this mode that give it its flavor or mood as some call it. Minor chords can be created out of these notes as well.

Lydian mode. Starts on the 4th note of the scale and is a major mode because it has a natural 3rd note but a sharp 4th. Major chords can be created out of this mode.

Mixolydian mode. Starts on the 5th note and is also a major mode because it has a natural third in it but has a flat 7th note. Dominant chords can go very well with this mode.

Study these modes thoroughly and see how they work with these chords I have mentioned. They will help you to understand why the modes are what they are and why they work well with certain chords.

Now let's look at the other two modes and see what they are. Major or minor?

Chapter 4 Modes Continued

Lesson 16: Aeolian mode (natural minor)

We now come to the sixth mode. The Aeolian mode. This mode is considered the natural minor mode because it consists of the flat 3rd, flat 6th, and flat 7th notes. These notes are to be flattened if you want to turn a major scale into a minor one.

Let me explain further.

Key of A major: A B C# D E F# G# A
$\qquad\qquad\qquad$ 1 2 3   4 5 6   7   8

To create the key of A minor, we need to flatten the 3rd, 6th, & 7th notes.

Key of A minor: A B C D E F G A
$\qquad\qquad\qquad$ 1 2 b3 4 5 b6 b7 8

We now have all natural notes in the A minor scale. This works with all 12 keys of the musical alphabet. So, if you ever want to turn a major scale into a minor one, just flatten these three notes.

We can also see very clearly that the A minor scale is made up of the same notes as the key of C major.

Key of C major: C D E F G A B C
$\qquad\qquad\qquad$ 1 2 3 4 5 6 7 8

Since this is the case, we can conclude that these two keys are relative.

The A minor is the relative minor to the key of C major. Why? Because they are made up of the same notes. It is this formula that makes up the Aeolian mode and naturally makes it a minor mode.

Like we learned earlier, if we start on the sixth note of the key of C (the A note) this is where we will play the Aeolian mode.

Aeolian mode in the key of C major:

A B C D E F G A
1 2 b3 4 5 b6 b7 8

As we learned before, the A major scale has three sharps. The C#, F#, & G#. But in order for the Aeolian mode to fit diatonically correct into the C major scale, these notes need to be flattened. Making this a minor mode.

Since we have the flat 3rd note, this tells us that this mode would sound great over minor chords or over a chord progression in a minor key. We can also see what chords we can create out of this mode as well.

We can create A minor, Amb6, Am7, Asus2, & Asus4. Any of these chords will sound good with this mode. If you'd like to know more about how modes work well with chords, I highly recommend you study chord theory. This will make this a lot easier to understand.

Since this is a course on modes for beginners I don't want to get too technical, but this is the basic fundamental principle of how modes and chords relate to each other.

Now let's look at the final mode, the Locrian mode.

Lesson 17: Locrian mode (diminished)

We now come to the 7th and final mode, the Locrian mode. This mode is very unique in the fact that it is not a major, or natural minor but a diminished mode.

When we take a major chord (any major chord) the 1 3 5 and we flatten the 3rd note it becomes a minor chord. If we flatten the 3rd and 5th note we create what is called a diminished chord. The Locrian mode is considered a diminished mode because it has both of these in it.

It is also the only mode that has the flat fifth note and that is what makes it unique compared to the others. Since it is the 7th mode it will start on the B note in the key of C major.

Locrian mode in the key of C major.

```
B  C  D  E  F  G  A  B
1  b2 b3 4  b5 b6 b7 8
```

In the key of B major, we have 5 sharps. C#, D#, F#, G#, & A#. As we can clearly see, these notes have been flattened to fit into the key of C major. Remember, all notes must fit correctly into the key that they come out of in order to sound correct.

This is why when people sometimes play music and you hear a bad note, it's not really a bad note it's just a note that doesn't naturally fit in the key that the music is written in. When all notes within a key are played correctly, the song sounds like music to the ears.

Even with minor chords and diminished chords that give music a sad somber mood, they can still fit nicely if placed properly within the right texture of a song. Let's look at the Locrian mode within another key.

Always remember what note the mode starts on in any key. It will always be the same position. The note will change but the position will stay the same. In the key of C major the Locrian mode is on the B because that is the 7th note.

In the key of G major it would be the F#, in the key of D major it will be on the C# note, and in the key of F it will be on the E note.

Locrian mode in the key of F major:

E F G A Bb C D E
1 b2 b3 4 b5 b6 b7 8

In the key of E major we naturally have 4 sharps. F#, G#, C#, & D#. In the key of F major all notes are natural except for the B flat.

Key of F major: F G A Bb C D E F

Since the Locrian mode consists of 5 flats, it fits perfectly within these two keys. Just like all the other modes and just like any other key that it is played in.

Can you figure out which chords can be created out of this mode?

Lesson 18: Natural minor

Although we have learned about this already, I wanted to touch base on it a bit more because it is very important to understand.   The reason for this is to fully comprehend what differentiates a major key from a minor key. And what differentiates a major key from its relative minor key.

For example, we look at the key of A major again and then turn it into an A minor key by making alterations to certain notes.

Notes in the key of A major:

A B C# D E F# G# A
1 2 3   4 5 6   7   8

When we flatten three of the 8 notes within the key we create the natural minor. The three notes that need to be flattened are the 3, 6, & 7 of the major key. In this case, the C#, F#, & G#. By flattening these three notes, we make them natural.

Notes in the key of A minor:

A B C D E F G A
1 2 b3 4 5 b6 b7 8

Since this is the note sequence in the Aeolian mode it is considered the natural minor mode.

42

What is great about the natural minor mode is that it can serve two purposes.

1. It lets us know what notes are needed to turn a major key into a minor key.
2. It lets us know what minor key is relative to its major.

For instance. The A minor scale is the natural minor of the key of A major, because they are both in A but some of the notes are different. So they produce similar sounds. They both have similar notes. Not all exact notes, but similar.

But if you look closely at the A minor scale, since all of the notes are natural and there are no sharps or flats, we can conclude that the key of A minor is "relative" to the Key of C major. Why? Once again, because the two keys consist of the same notes.

The A minor is the "natural" minor of A major, but the "relative" minor of C major. Make sense? This goes for all major keys. You will have a natural minor by flattening the three notes, but you will also have a relative minor to another major key.

This goes for all major keys. Look at the notes in any major key. Flatten the three notes needed to make the natural minor, then look at the notes and see which major key has the same ones. This will indicate the relative major key to the natural minor.

This will take a bit of a thought process, but if you write it out on a piece of paper as I have done in these examples, you'll discover the answers to the question of natural minor, and relative minor. And this will really help your guitar playing tremendously!

Lesson 19: Scale half steps

When studying the major and minor scales, you want to be aware of the half steps. This is important to know as well because it lets you know very quickly where certain modes are located and how the notes affect each other.

In the major scale, the half steps (one fret apart) will be between the 3 & 4 and the 7 & 8 notes. This goes for all major scales.

Key of C major: C D E F G A B C
                  1 2 3 4 5 6 7 8

Key of G major: G A B C D E F# G
                  1 2 3 4 5 6 7 8

Key of D major: D E F# G A B C# D
                  1 2 3 4 5 6 7 8

In these three major keys, even though the notes are different, the note intervals (distance between the notes) stay the same. They all have the Do Re Mi sound as well. But in the minor scale, this interval changes because of the flattened notes.

Key of C minor: C D Eb F G Ab Bb C
                  1 2 b3 4 5 b6 b7 8

Now the half steps are between the 2 & 3 and 5 & 6 notes. Remember this and you will be able to find your way around the fretboard easily.

Lesson 20: Five modes

The reason why it is important to be aware of the half steps in the major scale is that they directly relate to the 7 modes.

By knowing where the half steps are, you can easily find the modes that relate to those notes. The Phrygian mode is going to be right next to the Lydian mode, and the Locrian mode is going to be right next to the Ionian mode.

If you go back and look closely at the four modes you will see clearly that the Lydian mode has the same notes as the Phrygian mode except for the 3rd note.

The same goes with the Locrian mode. Since it is right next to the Ionian mode they share the same notes except for the 7th note that the Locrian mode starts on.

Go back and look at the modes, you will see this to be true. Since this is so, you could actually bring them down to five modes except for the one note difference in the Phrygian and Locrian modes that are located in the half step position.

So if you want to play the major Lydian mode you start on the 4th note of the major scale, but if you'd like to make it have a minor sound, just add the 3rd note to the mode where the Phrygian mode starts.

Same goes for the Ionian mode. If you want it to sound happy, play the Ionian major mode, but if you want it to have a darker diminished tone add the 7th note to the mode where the Locrian mode starts.

It is these half steps within the major scale that makes this possible. That is why it is important to know this. It actually makes learning the modes easier.

What is great about this one note difference in the half step position is the chords that can be created within each mode. If you need to, I would highly recommend you go back and review those lessons. They will really help you with practical application of the modes.

I'm trying to keep this as simple as possible so that you don't get overwhelmed with information like a lot of books tend to do, it's just that there is a lot you can do with the modes once you begin to understand how they work and why.

Chapter 4 Summary

In this chapter we have continued the modes and whether they are major or minor. We have also looked at the natural minor, scale half steps, and why you can bring them down to 5 modes.

<u>Aeolian mode.</u> This is your natural minor mode because it consists of the flat 3rd, 6th, & 7th notes. This makes any major key a natural minor. Be sure to remember this.

<u>Locrian mode</u>. This is the diminished mode because it has a flat 2nd, 3rd, 5th, 6th, & 7th. Diminished means you flatten the3rd and 5th. This is the only mode of all 7 that has the flat 3rd & 5th notes.

<u>The natural minor</u> is the Aeolian mode because of the notes that are flattened. We can also use this information to learn about the relative minor. A major and minor key that are made up of the same notes.

<u>Scale half steps </u>(one fret apart) are important to know as well because they allow you to locate certain modes very quickly since the notes are right next to each other.

<u>5 modes</u> can be easier to learn and are so because of the half step between the Phrygian and Lydian, and Locrian and Ionian. The notes in the modes are the same except for one, and it is that one note that can make all the difference.

Make sure you memorize what modes are major, minor and that the 7th is diminished. It will really help with playing over chords and staying in key

Chapter 5 Scale Mode Formulas

Lesson 21: Ionian mode formula

In the last few chapters we have learned that the modes all consist of the same notes within the key they are created from. But when the order of the notes are changed, the structure of the scale changes along with the chords that they relate to.

This is very important to comprehend because it lets us know what chords can be created out of each mode. This will give us insight into what mode to play over any particular chord. Like for instance, the Ionian, Lydian, and Mixolydian mode will work well over any major chord.

The Dorian mode would work well over a minor chord because of the flat third and flat seven that reside in the mode. And since the Mixolydian mode has a flat 7, it would work well over a dominant chord.

When the distance of the notes changes, the scale mode formula changes and it is a good idea to know what these scale formulas are for future reference. That is what we are going to look at in this chapter.

All seven modes consist of a series of whole steps and half steps. A whole step is the distance between two frets, and a half step is the distance between one fret. Remember the half steps we talked about earlier?

48

Ionian scale mode formula:

1 2 3 4 5 6 7 8
 W W H W W W H

In the Ionian mode we have a whole step between each note except for the 3 & 4, & 7 & 8. The reason for this is so that the notes of the scale line up correctly to produce the Do Re Mi sound we are so familiar with.

All 7 modes will have this, but since each one starts on a different note of the scale, the scale mode formula will be different for each mode. They will still consist of whole and half steps, but where these will be located within each mode will be different.

Key of C major:

C D E F G A B C
1 2 3 4 5 6 7 8
 W W H W W W H

Key of G major:

G A B C D E F# G
1 2 3 4 5 6 7 8
 W W H W W W H

As we can see, the key of G major has a F# and not a natural F. That is because the note has to fit into the correct interval (distance between two notes) sequence. Since the distance between the 6 & 7 is a whole step, this note has to be sharpened to fit properly.

Lesson 22: Dorian mode formula

The scale mode formula for the Dorian mode will be different because it starts on the second tone degree of the major scale it comes out of. As we learned earlier. It will still have the whole steps and half steps because the notes are the same, they'll just be lined up differently.

Key of C Dorian mode:

```
D   E   F   G   A   B   C   D
1   2  b3   4   5   6  b7   8
W   H   W   W   W   H   W
```

Since the Dorian mode starts on the D note of the key of C major we can see very clearly that the whole & half steps stay the same, but they are now in a different location.

Since this is a minor mode, we can see that the half steps are now located between the 2 & 3 and the 6 & 7. Even though the notes are the same as the Ionian mode, since the mode starts on D instead of C it changes the mood of the scale.

All seven modes will use the same notes of the key they come from, but since they all start on different notes, they will have a different mode formula expressing a different emotion.

50

Key of G Dorian mode:

A B C D E F# G A
1 2 b3 4 5 6 b7 8
W H W W W H W

Here we can see with the Dorian mode in the key of G major, the scale mode formula is the same as in C major. This will with all Dorian modes in any key you choose to play it in.

Key of A Dorian mode:

B C# D E F# G# A B
1 2 b3 4 5 6 b7 8
W H W W W H W

In the key of E major we have three sharps and these must be present in the scale. Since we are playing the Dorian mode we start on the B note and we can see that the scale mode formula is the same as the other two keys C & G.

The sharps are still present but just in a different order. And since this is the same with each key, we can clearly see that the mode will always have a flat third and a flat seven.

This will allow us to figure out very easily what minor chords will work with this mode by knowing the chord formula.

Lesson 23: Phrygian mode formula

The next mode in line is the Phrygian mode that starts on the 3rd note of the major key it comes out of. Since we are working with the key of C major we will continue with this key. But remember, this can be applied to all keys in the musical spectrum.

The Phrygian mode is quite interesting because not only does it have a flat third and seventh note, but it also has a flat 2 and flat 6th. This gives it a different type of minor mood than the Dorian because of these two extra flat notes.

Key of C Phrygian mode:

```
E  F  G  A  B  C  D  E
1 b2 b3  4  5 b6 b7  8
H  W  W  W  H  W  W
```

Once again, the key of E major has four sharps, but to line up diatonically correctly with the Phrygian mode in the key of C major, the notes need to be flattened. If we flatten the 2, 3, 6, & 7th notes, we now have the E Phrygian mode in the key of C major.

Remember, it doesn't matter what note you start on, they must conform to the key that they come out of. That is why the mode formula changes with each mode.

We can see from looking at the scale mode formula, that it has changed from the Ionian and Dorian. Although we still have two half steps in the scale, they have moved to a different position. They now reside between the 1 & 2, and the 5 & 6.

It is this placement of the half steps that give this mode its character or mood. And like the other two modes, the formula will be the same in each key.

Key of B Phrygian mode:

```
D#  E   F#  G#  A#  B   C#  D
1   b2  b3  4   5   b6  b7  8
  H   W   W   W  H   W   W
```

In the key of B major we have 5 sharps. C#, D#, F#, G#, & A#. SInce the Phrygian mode is our third mode, it starts on the the third note of the B major scale which is the D# note. When we start it here, we can see that it has the same formula as the other keys presented.

It consists of the flat 2, 3, 6, & 7. This clearly tells us that it is a minor mode and would work well over minor chords. Remember, scales and chords work together best when they come out of the same key, and this is why you want to know this information.

If you know what mood you are trying to convey when you play the modes and you know what the mode formula is, it will help you to choose what chords to play them with. If it is a major mode (like the Ionian) it is major chords that will sound good. Dorian or Phrygian, choose minor chords.

Lesson 24: Lydian mode formula

Now we come to the fourth mode in the sale, the Lydian mode. Do you remember if this is a major or a minor? Wel, let's take a look. The scale mode formula will tell us very quickly.

Key of C Lydian mode:

```
F  G  A   B  C  D   E   F
1  2  3  #4 5  6   7   8
W  W  W  H  W  W  H
```

Since the F note is the fourth of C major, the Lydian mode will start here. In the key of F, we have a Bb and for the note in the mode to conform to the key of C major, we need to sharpen it. We can also see that the half steps have also moved to a different location.

They are now between the 4 & 5, and 7 & 8. Since this mode has no flat third, we can conclude that it is a major mode and will work well with major chords. We now have two modes that will work well with major chords, the Ionian and the Lydian.

Key of D Lydian mode:

```
G  A  B  C#  D  E  F#  G
1  2  3  #4  5  6  7   8
 W  W  W   H  W  W  H
```

54

In the key of D major we have two sharps. The C#, and F#. And since there is a whole step between the 3 & 4, we can see that the mode has a sharp four in it. Same as with the key of C major or any other major key. Once again, no flat third note.

So we can conclude that this mode will work well with major chords such as D major, Dm7, Dm6, Dm9, Dm6/9, and even a Dsus4. If you study chord formulas like I've touched on in previous lessons, you will see that all these chords can be created out of this mode.

Key of A Lydian mode:

```
D  E  F#  G#  A  B  C#  D
1  2  3   #4  5  6  7   8
W  W  W   H   W  W  H
```

Same goes for the key of A major. Fourth note is the D and that is where we play the Lydian mode. The sharp fourth is present as well as the natural third. And the half steps are in the same location as the other keys.

This is the "secret" of knowing these magical mode formulas. They allow you to know how to mix and match. Vey much like putting a square peg in a square hole or a round peg in a round hole.

This is where guitar players run into problems sounding good when they play solos and melody lines. They start trying to put a square peg in a round hole and it doesn't fit. By knowing your mode formulas, you will eliminate this every time.

Lesson 25: Mixolydian mode formula

We now come to the fifth mode in the scale, the mixolydian mode. This mode will start on the fifth note of the scale. This will be another major mode. Do you remember why? Well, let's take a look.

Key of C Mixolodian mode:

```
G  A  B  C  D  E  F   G
1  2  3  4  5  6  b7  8
W  W  H  W  W  H  W
```

Like before we can see that to conform to the key of C major we need to flatten the F note which is normally sharp in the key of G major. In doing so, we can see that this is a major mode because it has no flat third note. Although it does have a flat 7th.

This could even be thought of as a dominant mode because of the fact that it only has one change and that's the b7. The b7 is considered dominant in chords so that might be a good way of remembering this mode formula.

Once you learn your chord formulas (1 3 5, etc) you will be able to clearly see all the chords that can come out of this mode and all the other ones. It is really amazing how many different chords these modes work with.

This mode will work very well with major and dominant chords. And we know this because of the scale mode formula. It even tells us that we could create a B diminished chord out of it (1 b3 b5) because the notes are in the mode.

56

Whatever chord notes are in the mode, can be created out of it. And since the mode and chords come from the same place, that tells us that they can play together nicely. Here's something you can try, create a chord that comes out of any particular mode, record it on your phone and then play the mode over it. You'll see that they sound good together.

Key of A Mixolydian mode:

E F# G# A B C# D E
1 2   3   4 5 6   b7 8
   W   W   H W W H   W

In addition to seeing that there is a flat seven in the mode no matter what key we choose to play it in, we can also see once again, that the half steps have moved from the Lydian mode and are now between the 3 & 4 & 7 & 8.

It is this scale mode formula that allows us to see that it has a flat seven, that it is a major mode, and that a multitude of chords can be created out of it that the mode (any mode) will work well with. Never forget this.

That is why they say that music is a science of mathematics. Because it deals with formulas (chord and scale formulas) and it deals with numbers that create those formulas. Kind of like ingredients to a secret sauce.

No matter what key you choose to play the mixolydian mode out of, it will always start on the 5th note of the scale and consist of a flat seven. It will be a major mode because it does not have a flat third. Only a flat seven. Just like a dominant chord.

Chapter 5 summary

In this chapter we have looked at the scale mode formula for the first five modes. This is important to know because it clearly spells out where the half stapes are located, and what chords can be played out of each mode.

Understanding the whole step half step formula in all seven modes will help you to create it quickly, see where the half steps are and figure out what chords are best to play it with. This can be essential in songwriting.

Ionian mode is a major mode with the scale formula W-W-H-W-W-W-H.

Dorian mode is a minor mode with the scale formula W-H-W-W-W-H-W.

Phrygian mode is a minor mode with the formula H-W-W-W-H-W-W.

Lydian mode is a major mode with the formula W-W-W-H-W-W-H.

Mixolydian mode is a major mode with the formula W-W-H-W-W-W-H.

When you look at them lined up this way it is easy to reference what the formulas are for each mode. Make sure you study this and commit it to memory if possible. It will really help you to see what chords can be played with each mode.

Let's look at the other two scale mode formulas.

Chapter 6 Mode Formulas Continued

Lesson 26: Aeolian mode formula

Now we come to the natural minor mode. Like we learned in previous lessons, this is considered a natural minor because of the mode formula. It is structured in such a way that we create the natural minor. This is done by flattening the 3rd, 6th, and 7th of any major scale.

Since the notes in this mode naturally line up that way, it is considered the natural minor mode. It could also be considered a relative minor mode because the notes of the two scales are the same.

Key of C Aeolian mode:

```
A  B  C  D  E  F  G  A
1  2  b3 4  5  b6 b7 8
W  H  W W  H  W  W
```

What I mean by relative is that the key of C major consists of the same notes as A minor. It is this Aeolian mode formula that makes this a minor mode. Because it has a flat third in it. Since it also has a flat 6 & 7, it is considered a natural minor mode. Unlike the Dorian and Phrygian modes that are minor also.

Since they don't have the flat 6 and 7th notes they are only considered minor but not natural minor. It is the flattening of the 6th and 7th notes that makes the natural minor. A very important concept to understand and remember.

Let's look again at the key of C major and C minor.

Key of C major: C D E F G A B C

Key of C minor: C D Eb F G Ab Bb C

In the key of C minor we have flattened the 3rd, 6th, & 7th notes. This creates the natural C minor scale. But since the Aeolian mode in the key of C major is played at the 6th note (the A) then the A minor scale is created. A B C D E F G.

In the key of A major we have three sharps. You can see that they have been flattened to fit diatonically correct into the C major scale. So this creates the A minor scale. Since it has the same notes as the C major, it is considered relative.

C major scale: C D E F G A B C

A minor scale: A B C D E F G A

Same notes. See how it is considered relative? Now the C minor scale is the natural minor because the notes are similar to the C major scale and both scales are in the key of C.

We can also see the location of the half steps have once again changed. They are now between the 2 & 3, & 5 & 6 notes. Since this is another minor mode, we can easily play it over minor chords. But also play it over C major chords because it has the same notes.

Lesson 27: Locrian mode formula

We now come to the last of the seven modes. The Locrian mode. The diminished mode. This mode is unique in the fact it is the only one of the seen modes that has a flat fifth note. This flat fifth note is what gives it a character unlike the other modes.

In order to make a major triad (the 1 3 5) into a diminished triad we need to flatten both the 3rd and the 5th notes. The chord formula would then be a 1 b3 b5. In the key of C the notes would be C, Eb, & Gb.

And since this is the seventh mode, we would play it at the 7th note of the scale.

Key of C Locrian mode:

```
B  C   D  E  F  G   A   B
1  b2  b3 4  b5 b6  b7  8
 H   W   W H  W   W   W
```

Since the B and C are naturally next to each other in the musical alphabet, we can conclude that the half step will be right at the start of the mode. And since the major scale formula is always two whole steps, one half step and then three whole steps, it is pretty easy to see where the next one is.

Can you see that the major scale formula is always in the same order? It just seems to change because it starts on a different note for each mode.

In fact, when you really look at the formula, the half steps in the key of C major (no matter what mode you are playing) will always be between the B & C & E & F. So you just need to know where these notes are located within the mode and you can easily find them.

Same goes with any other key you choose to play the modes in. Wherever the half steps are in the Ionian mode, they will be in the same place as the others. Let's take a look.

Key of F Locrian mode:

```
E  F   G  A  Bb  C   D   E
1  b2  b3 4  b5  b6  b7  8
H  W   W  H  W   W   W
```

Once again we see that the half step is between the 1 & 2 and again between the 4 & 5. We can also see that the sharps in the key of E major have been flattened to fit into the key of F major. And since the key of F major has one flat (Bb) it is still present.

In this key, the half step falls between the E & F and the A & Bb notes. This will be the same for all 7 modes in this key.

The scale mode formula is important to know for all the reasons stated throughout these two chapters. But the main thing it does is tell you what sharps or flats will be present within any major key.

Remember, the Locrian mode is the diminished mode as it has a flat 3rd and flat 5th. Along with the flat 6th, and 7th. This mode can work well over many, many minor and diminished chords. I highly recommend you study chord theory to fully understand this.

Lesson 28: Mode chord examples

In the previous lesson I showed some chords that can be created out of knowing the mode formula. Now I'd like to go into detail a bit further. I'd like to give you a few examples to get you started working with chords in each mode.

As I stated before, it is best to study chord theory to fully understand this material on chord construction. Since this is a beginner book and there are literally thousands of chords that can be created on the guitar, I'll only present a few in each mode to get you started.

This will keep things simple and easy to understand. We will look at each mode and pick a few chords that can be derived from them and then if you want, you can take it from there. I will keep it simple and not overwhelm you with too much theory.

Modes are geared toward creating guitar solos and melody. But just like with any scales you learn in the future, they relate to chords and the better you understand this, the better you'll be able to play the modes.

<u>Ionian mode</u> in the key of C major:

C D E F G A B C
1 2 3 4 5 6 7 8

C major-C E G, CM6-C E G A , CM7-C E G B, Csus4-C F G.
      1 3 5   1 3 5 6   1 3 5 7   1 4 5

Can you see how we get these chords out of this mode?

When it comes to chords, any two or more notes played together can be considered a chord. A power chord (most commonly played in rock music) is a chord of the 1 & 5. A triad is made up of the 1 3 5 and an extended chord will be created with notes that go beyond that.

We can create even more chords if we use one of the other notes as the root note. Like for instance the D note.

D minor D F A, Dm6 D F A B, Dm7 D F A C, Dsus4 D G A.
      1 b3 5   1 b3 5 6   1 b3 5 7   1 4 5

Since the F is normally sharp in the key of D major and it is flattened in the Ionian mode in the key of C major, we can create minor chords. And if we did this with every note as the root, we could create a lot more chords within this mode.

<u>Dorian mode</u> in the key of G major:

A B C D E F# G A
1 2 b3 4 5 6 b7 8

A minor-A C E, Am6-A C E F#, Am7-A C E G, Asus4-A D E.
      1 b3 5   1 b3 5 6   1 b3 5 b7   1 4 5

If you look closely, we could even create a D major triad because of the notes that are in this mode. We just need to use the D as the root (the 1) of the chord. Can you see what I mean?

<u>Phrygian mode</u> in the key of C major:

E F G A B C D E
1 b2 b3 4 5 b6 b7 8

This mode has the flattened 3rd so we know the chords will be minor in the key of E.

E minor-E G B, Emb6-E G B C, Em7-E G B D, Esus4-E A B.
      1 b3 5   1 b3 5 b6   1 b3 5 b7   1 4 5

<u>Lydian mode</u> in the key of G major
C D E F# G A B C
1 2 3 #4 5 6 7 8

Once again, we can create chords in C. C major, CM6, CM7, although since we now have a sharp 4th note we can't create the Csus4 chord. Although, we could create the Csus2 (1 2 5) C D G.

<u>Mixolydian mode</u> in the key of A major:

E F# G# A B C# D E
1 2 3 4 5 6 b7 8

Here we have the mode with the flat 7th note. Since we have a natural third, this lets us know what kind of chords we can easily create in the key of E.

E major- E G# B, EM6-E G# B C#, E7-E G# B D, EM6b7-E G# B C# D.
      1 3 5   1 3 5 6   1 3 5 b7   1 3 5 6 b7

Since the 7th note is flattened in this mode but the 3rd is natural it tells us that the chords in E would be either major or dominant. Can you see how important the placement of the 3rd note is? Like how it determines major, minor, or sus?

We can also see very clearly that if we used the A note as the root we could create A major chords. But if we used the B note as the root we could create B minor chords because the D (flat 7th in the mode) would normally be sharp in the key of B major.

Aeolian mode in the key of B major:

```
G  A  B  C  D  E  F  G
1  2  b3 4  5  b6 b7 8
```

Since this is our natural minor mode and has the flat 3rd note, we already know that the chords we can create in G are going to be minor. G minor, Gm6, Gm7, etc.

Locrian mode in the key of F major

```
E  F  G  A  B  C  D  E
1  b2 b3 4  b5 b6 b7 8
```

Last but not least our diminished mode. Here we can create diminished chords in E because of the flat 3rd, and 5th notes. We can also conclude that we can create minor 7th chords in E because of the flat 7th note.

```
E diminished-E  G  B,  Edimb6-E  G  B  C,  Edimb7-E G  B D,
            1 b3 b5              1 b3 b5 b6            1 b3 b5 b7
```

As I mentioned before, many, many more chords can be created out of these modes. In fact, if you use each of the 7 notes as a root note, you could create a whole book of chords.

This is the whole purpose of knowing the scale mode formula for each mode. Because it tells you a wealth of information.

1. What sharps or flats are in a key
2. Where the half steps reside in each mode
3. If it is a major or minor mode
4. What chords can be easily created out of each one

In this lesson I have given you a few chords that you can create in each mode to keep things simple, but if you really dive in you'll find a lot more that can be created within each mode.

This is important to know because if you write songs and want to stay in key when playing a guitar solo or melody line and you know what chords go with each mode, you'll sound good every time. You'll amaze your friends and family with your awesome guitar skills.

But in order to do so you must study. Study and put this information into practice. It is one thing to know this in theory, but it is something else to be able to put it into practical application. That is where the rubber meets the road so to speak.

Lesson 29: Mode chord progressions

Now that we know some chords that we can play out of the modes, we can put them together to create chord progressions. These will be useful for soloing over and listening for how the chords and modes sound in harmony with each other.

For this example I will use the key of C major to keep things simple. But remember, it works the same in all keys. I recommend you should try it in different ones to fully understand how the concept works.

Ionian mode in C major: C D E F G A B C (major)

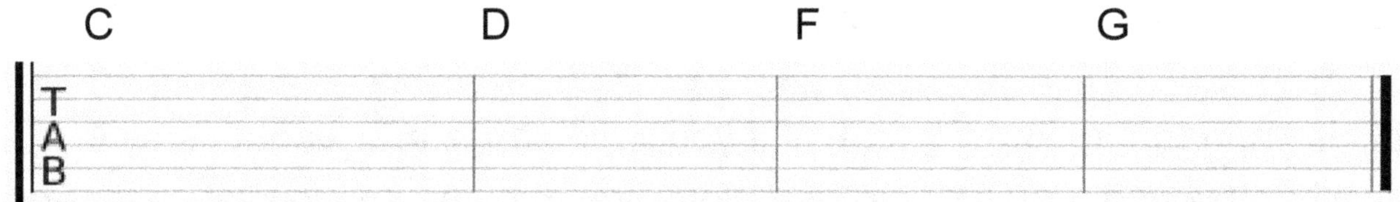

Dorian mode in C major: D E F G A B C D (minor b3 & b7)

Phrygian mode in C major: E F G A B C D E (minor b2, b3, b6, & b7)

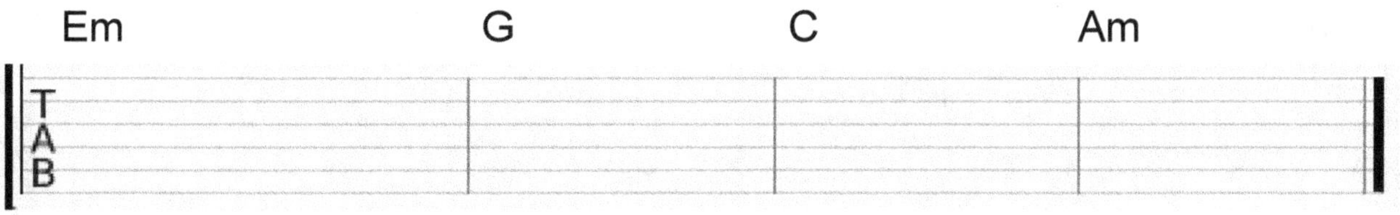

Em   G   C   Am

Lydian mode in C major: F G A B C D E F (major #4)

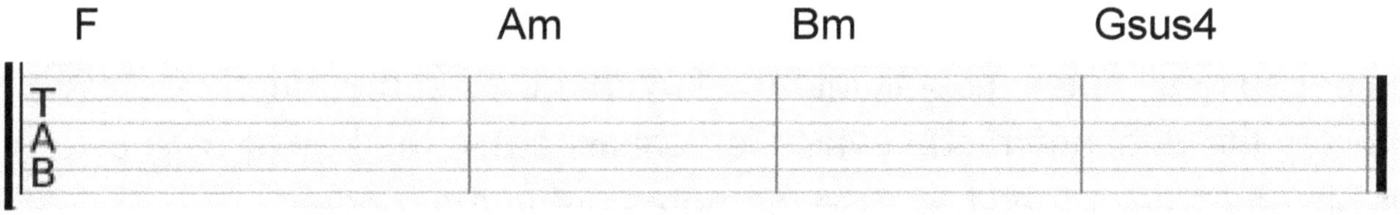

F   Am   Bm   Gsus4

Mixolydian mode in C major: G A B C D E F G (major b7)

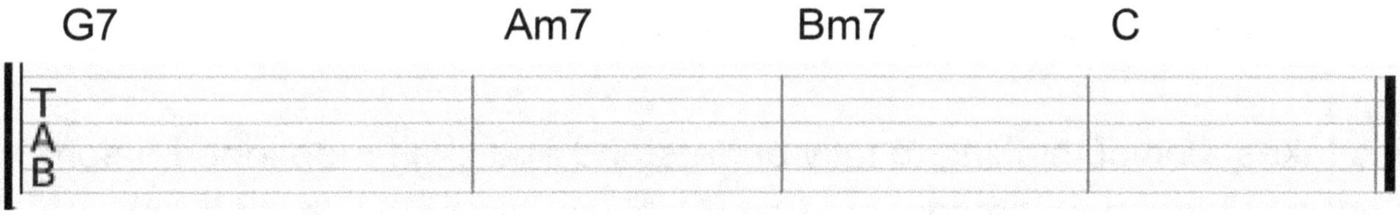

G7   Am7   Bm7   C

Aeolian mode in C major: A B C D E F G A (natural minor b3, b6, & b7)

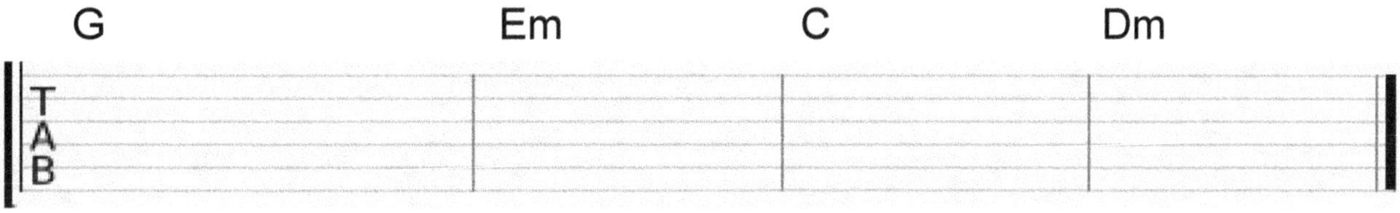

G   Em   C   Dm

Locrian mode in C major: B C D E F G A B (diminished b3, 5, 6, & 7)

Bdim	C	Dm	Am

```
T
A
B
```

Can you see how all these chords can be played within each of these modes? Can you also see how you can create major chords in a minor mode and vica versa?

It is because all notes must fit into the key that they come out of. So even if you play the B locrian mode (which is diminished) in the key of C, you can still play a C major triad because the notes are in the mode.

Although when it comes to the D triad, it must be minor because the F note is natural and not sharp like it would be in a D major triad.

Make sense? If not, go back through the lesson.

This takes a bit of thinking to fully understand and like I mentioned before, to get a full grasp of the concept you might want to study chord theory. You can do this with my book <u>Rhythm Guitar Alchemy</u>. This shows you the science of chords and how to use it to improve your rhythm playing

Lesson 30: Finger dexterity development

When it comes to playing modes and solos in general, you want to make sure to get your hands and fingers in shape. As you know by now, a lot of the spacing in the modes is three notes per string. And when you link the modes together (as I will show you in the next chapter) it will help to have your fingers ready to take on the challenge.

In this lesson we are going to look at some finger exercises that will help to develop your fingers so that they can play some cool licks within the modes as well as the chords that we learned earlier.

With these dexterity exercises, make sure to use all four fingers. If you're not used to playing with the pinky that's fine. These exercises will help you develop it. It will be beneficial for playing the modes with style.

Exercise #1

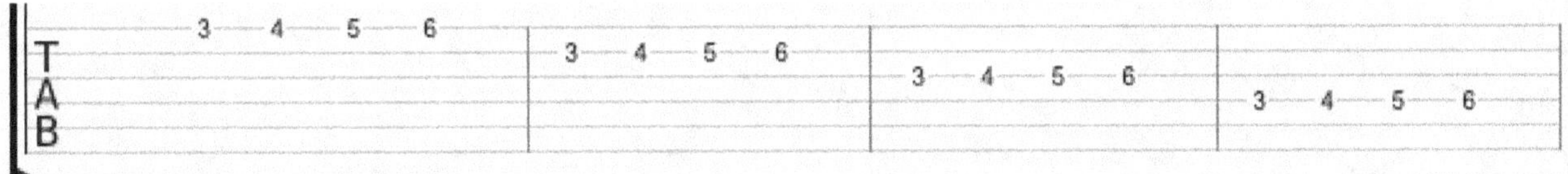

Exercise #2

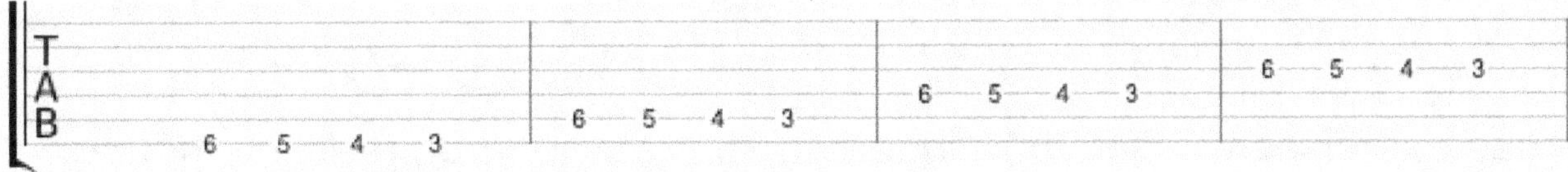

Exercise #3

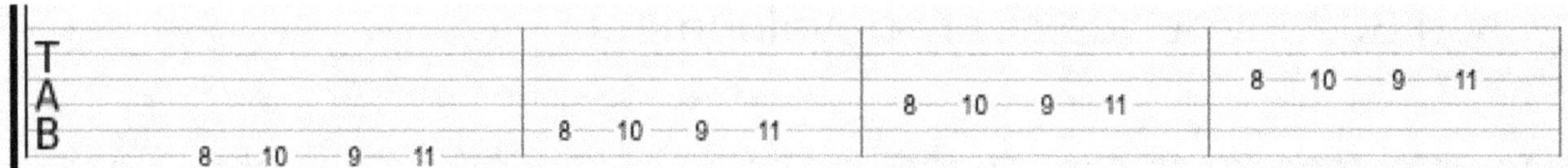

Exercise #4

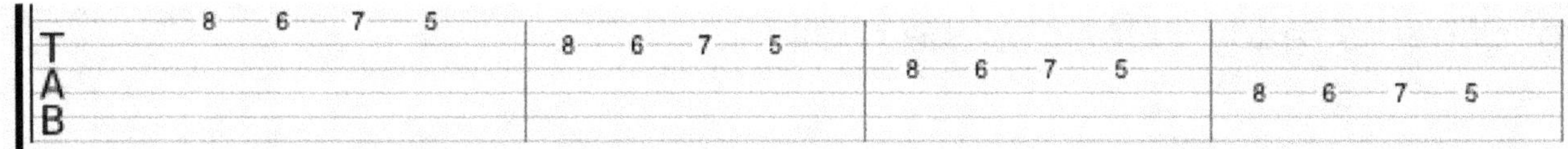

Exercise #5

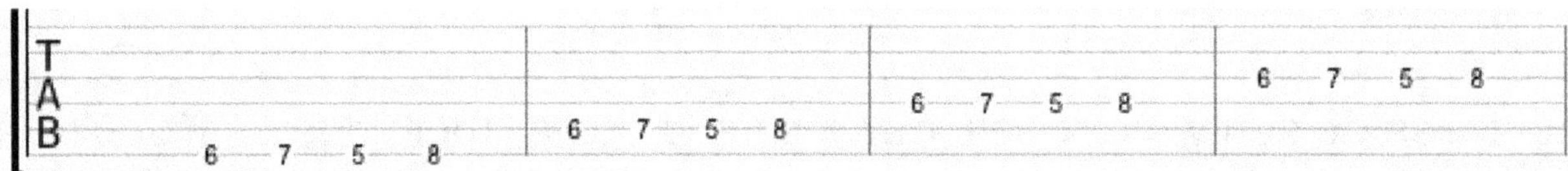

Exercise #6

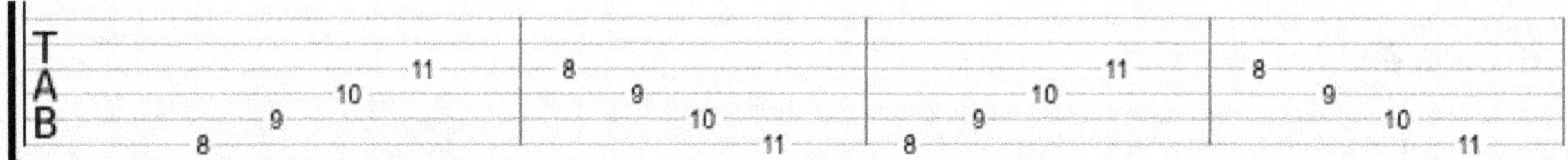

Exercise #7

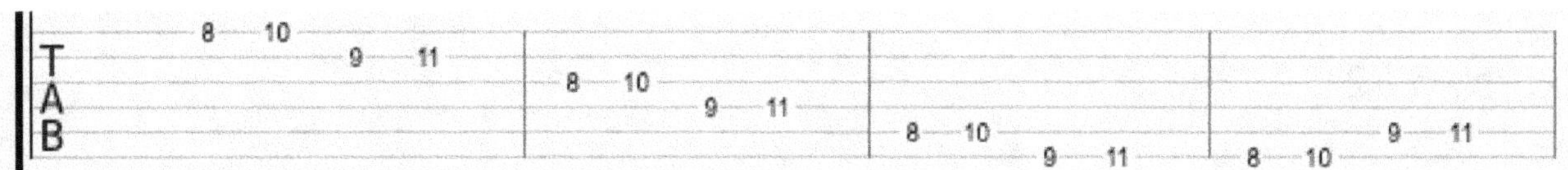

These exercises will get your fingers in shape when you practice them on a daily basis. As you go through them you will discover more. Start off by picking downward on each note, then work at picking each note up and down.

Alternate picking will help you to develop speed and accuracy.

Chapter 6 Summary

In this chapter we have covered some very important aspects of playing modes on the guitar. The first two lessons continue from the previous chapter and the next three bring in some new concepts.

Aeolian mode is a minor mode with the scale formula W H W W H W W

Locrian mode is diminished with the scale formula H W W H W W W

Mode chord examples. These are the chords that can be made out of each mode. Since each mode has a different character, different chords can be created.

Mode chord progressions. Once you learn what types of chords can be played in each mode, you want to then put them together to create chord progressions. This will help you to understand and hear how they work well with each mode.

Finger dexterity exercises. These are what will help you to execute the modes more thoroughly. The better your hands and fingers are in shape, the better you will be able to play the modes, chords and guitar licks that reside within them.

Make sure to study the mode formulas and know them by heart. Make sure to study the chords that can be created out of each mode as this will help you with being able to stay in key when soloing.

And remember, to work on your finger exercises daily. I nice hand and finger warm up will work wonders for aspects of guitar playing. Not just modes.

Chapter 7 Licks Within The Modes

Lesson 31: Why guitar licks are important

Now we come to the really fun part if you ask me. How to put the notes of the modes into practical application from a guitar solo point of view.

Until now, we have been looking at them from a theoretical point of view. Learning the notes, formulas, chords and how to put this all together in a rhythm sense. Now we look at how to play guitar licks for soloing.

When it comes to guitar solos, they are composed of guitar licks that reside within the scales that they come out of. It starts with the notes in the scale and continues with techniques such as hammer-ons, pull-offs, bends, trills, slides, vibrato, etc.

You mix and match these ingredients to create a secret sauce that becomes unique to you and your style of playing. But before we can do that we need to learn about these musical concepts.

For it is these concepts and techniques that will bring the scales to life. This will make them sound less mechanical. When playing guitar solos it's not just enough to know the notes, you must know how to execute them in such a way to make them sound musical.

This is what we will learn in this chapter. How to bring the 7 modes to life when playing them during a guitar solo.

Hammer-on

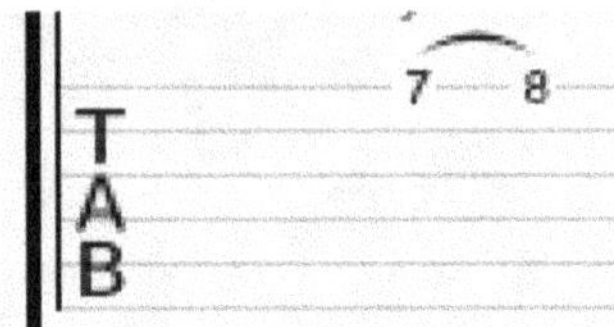

Place one finger on a note and hammer-on to the next with your second finger. Pick the 7th fret and hammer-on to the 8th.

Pull-off

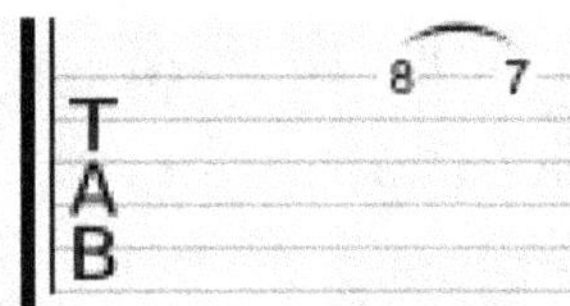

This is the opposite. Place two fingers down on the 7th & 8th frets. Pick the 8th fret and pull-off back to the 7th.

Bends

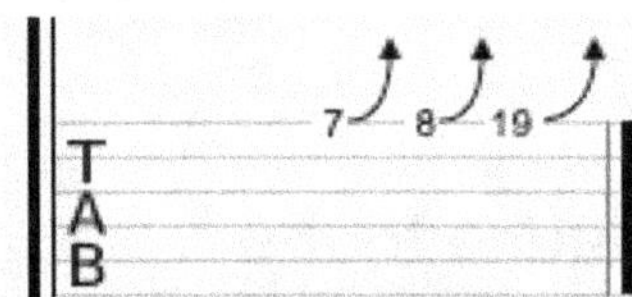

You pick a note and bend it up. In this example, you pick the 7the fret and bend up. Then proceed to do the same with the 8th & 10th frets.

Slides

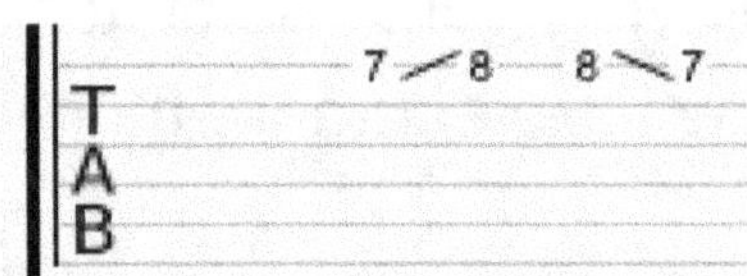

Pick a note and either slide up or down to the next note. Here are two examples. Slide up from the 7 to the 8 or Slide down from the 8 to the 7.

Vibrato

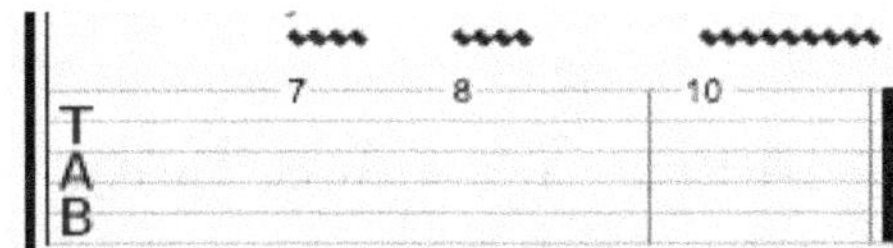

You pick a note and gently vibrate it up and down. This creates a vibrato effect that is very similar to a singer's vocal cords vibrating.

Trills

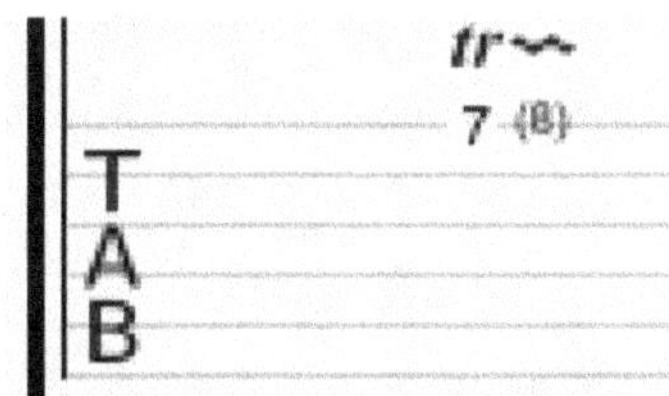

You pick a note and hammer-on, pull-off the next note repeatedly. Here you pick the 7th fret and repeatedly hammer-on, pull-of the 8th fret.

There are more to these techniques then just this, but these will get you started working with them. There are also more techniques used in lead guitar playing but these ones are the most common. As you head in this direction you will discover more.

Remember, guitar licks are important because that is what guitar solos are made up of. Very much like a paragraph is written up of sentences that are made up of words with individual letters. Same thing applies here. If you look at this way it will make a lot more sense in the long run.

Take some time and practice these techniques and get familiar with them. As you do, you'll begin to recognize them in songs and solos that inspire you to play.

Lesson 32: Ionian mode guitar licks

The first mode in any key as we know is the Ionian mode. To make things more interesting I am going to present it in different places along the fretboard. This will help you to play it in different keys.

Ionian mode guitar lick in the key of G major

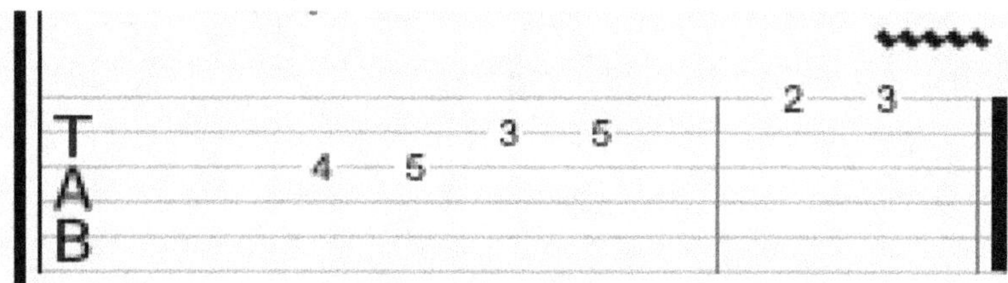

Here is a nice run on three strings with a vibrato on the end note.

Ionian mode guitar lick in the key of B major

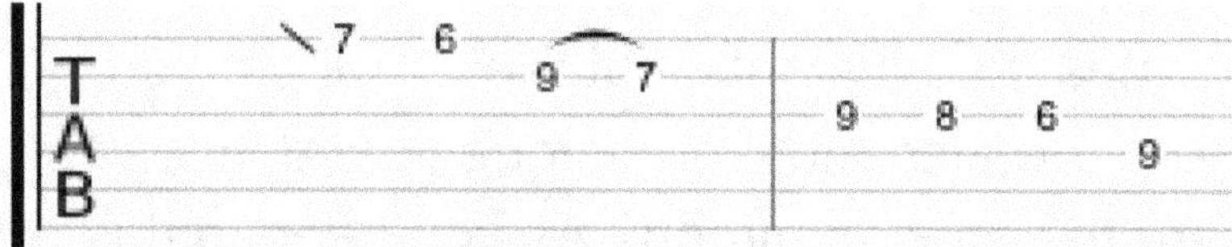

Here we slide into the 7th fret and add a pull-off from the 9 to the 7th fret on the 2nd string.

Ionian mode guitar lick in the key of A major

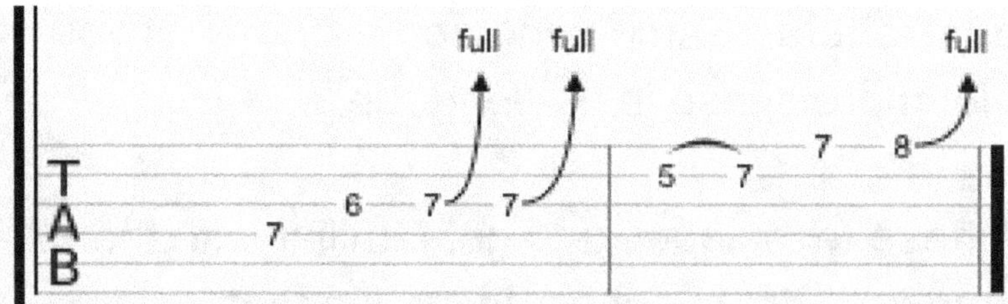

Here we use bends on the 7th fret of the third string and a pull-off on the 5th fret of the second string and end with another bend on the 8th.

Ionian mode guitar lick in the key of C major

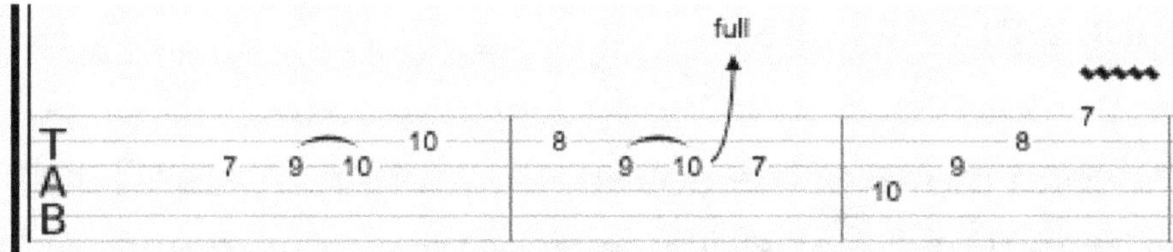

A simple lick that incorporates hammer-ons at the 9th fret third string with a bend added on the second one, and a vibrato at the end on the 7th fret first string.

Ionian mode guitar lick in the key of E major

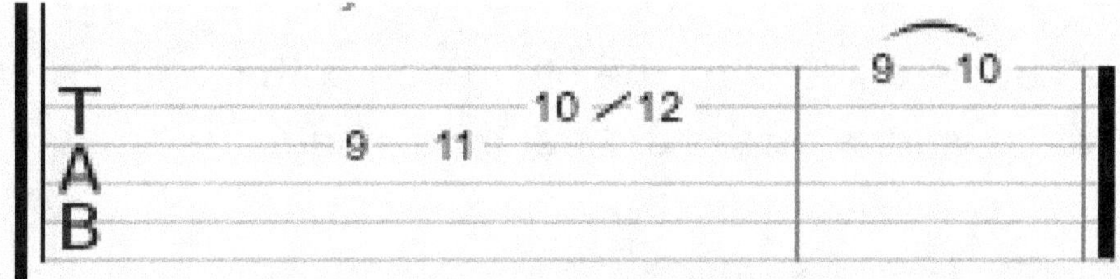

Here we start with a pull-off at the 14th fret and proceed through the lick, add another pull-off at the 13th fret and end with a vibrato.

Ionian mode guitar lick in the key of D major

Here is a simple lick that incorporates a slide at the 10th fret second string and a hammer-on at the 9th fret first string.

Each of these licks can be played within the Ionian mode in any key you choose.

Lesson 33: Dorian mode guitar licks

We now move into the second mode of the seven, the Dorian mode. This is a minor mode so it will give us a bit of a different feel than the Ionian. Let's take a look at some guitar licks that reside within this mode.

Dorian mode guitar lick in the key of C major

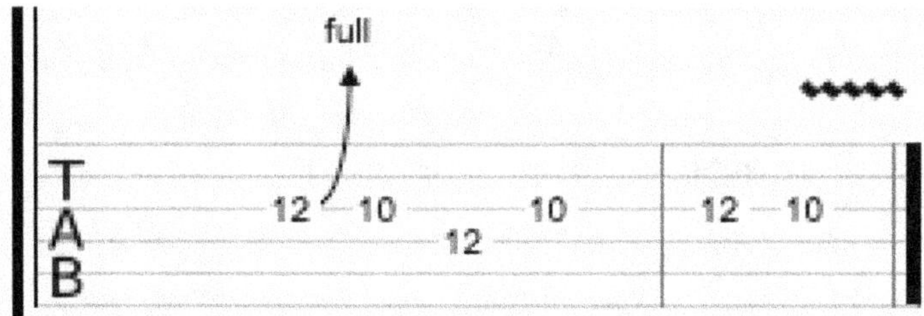

Here we start with a bend at the 12th fret third string and end the lick with a vibrato at the 10th fret of the third string.

Dorian mode guitar lick in the key of F major

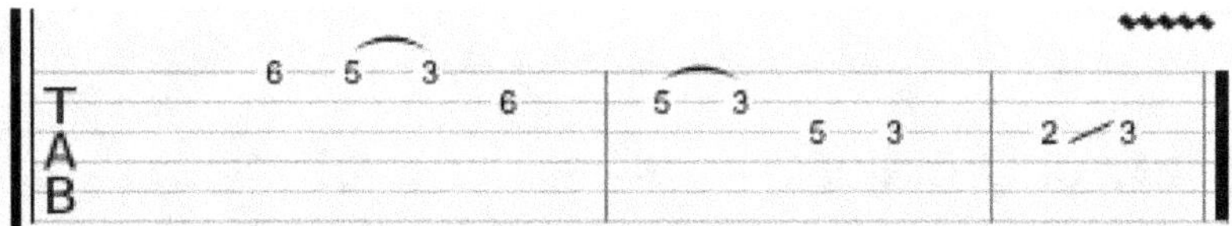

Here is a nice run with a couple pull-offs off the 5th fret on both the first and second strings ending with a vibrato on the 3rd fret third string.

Dorian mode guitar lick in the key of A major

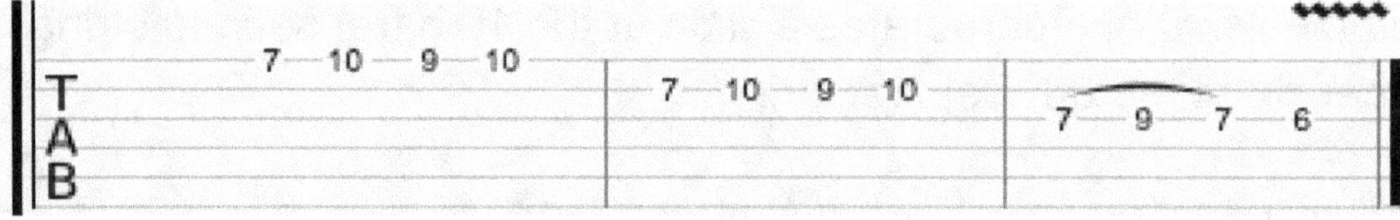

This guitar lick is pretty straightforward with a nice hammer-on pull-off at the 7th fret third string ending with a vibrato on the 6th fret third string.

Dorian mode guitar lick in the key of B

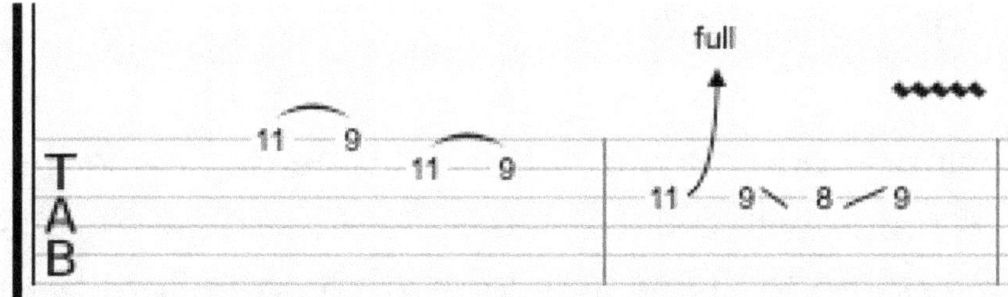

Here we have two pull-offs at the 11th fret on the first and second strings, followed by a bend at the 11th fret third string. Then proceeding to a couple slides down and up at the 9th fret ending with a vibrato back on the 9th fret.

Dorian mode guitar lick in the key of G major

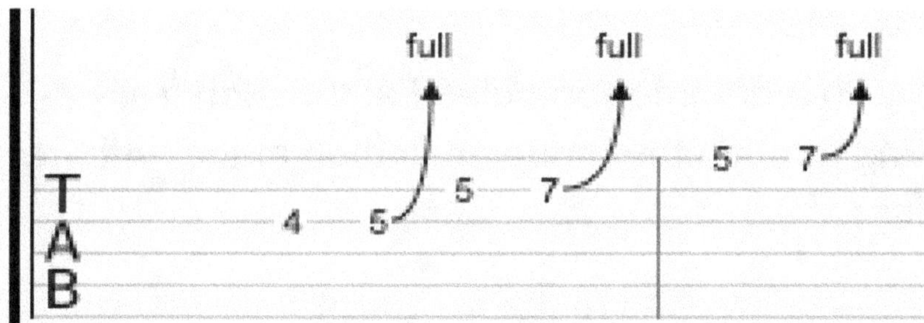

Here we have a simple guitar lick utilizing bends at the 5th fret third string, 7th fret second string and the 7th fret first string. Nice lick to practice your string bends.

Dorian mode guitar lick in the key of D major

Here is a nice lick that utilizes the pull-off at the 12th fret on the first and second strings while finishing with a vibrato at the 12th fret on the second string.

Lesson 34: Phrygian mode guitar licks

Now we come to the other minor mode played at the 3rd tone degree in the scale, the Phrygian mode. A mode with a flat 2, flat 3, flat 6, and flat 7. It is these notes that make it a minor mode. Now let's look at some guitar licks we can create within it.

Phrygian mode guitar lick in the key of C major

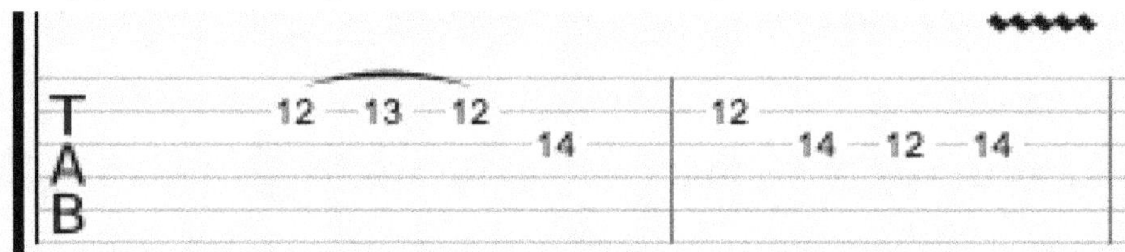

Here is another lick starting with a hammer-on pull-off at the 12th fret second string and progressing through the mode ending on at the 14th fret with vibrato on the third string.

Phrygian mode guitar lick in the key of F major

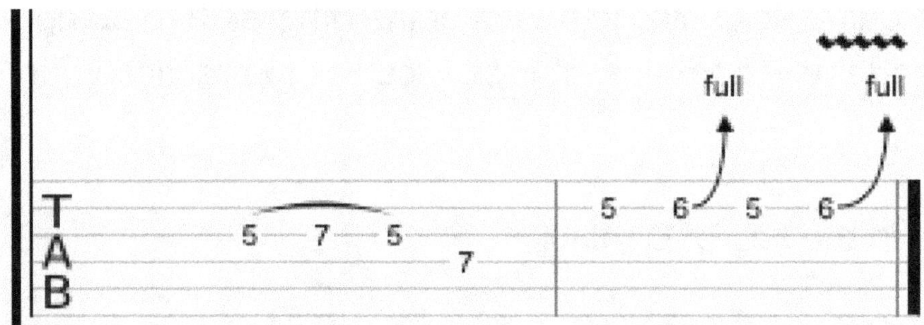

Here is a nice simple lick starting off with a hammer-on pull-off at the 5th fret third string and progressing to a couple bends at the 6th fret on the second string ending with a nice vibrato added to the last bend.

Phrygian mode guitar lick in the key of D major

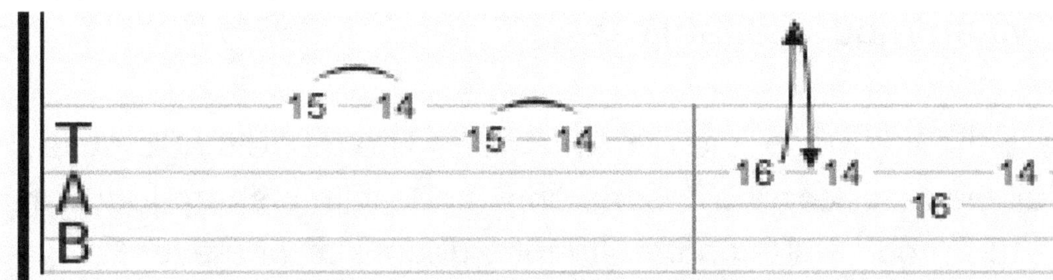

Here is a nice lick that starts with a couple pull-offs at the 15th fret on the first and second strings. Then proceeds with a bend-release at the 16th fret third string followed by a three note finish at the 14th fret third string.

Phrygian mode guitar lick in the key of A major

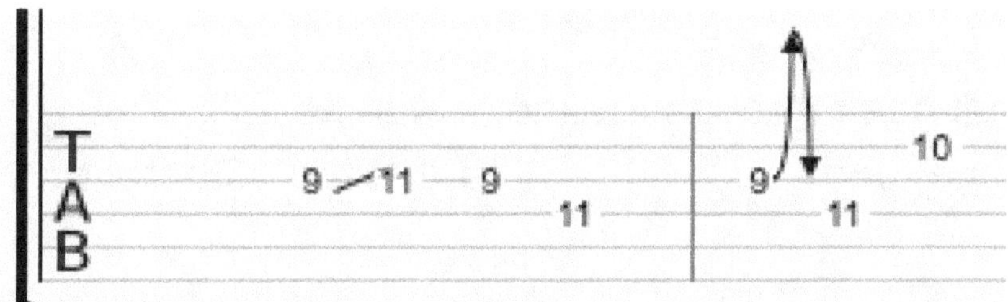

Here is a nice lick starting out with a slide at the 9th fret third string followed by a couple notes before the bend-release is presented at the 9th fret third string. Ending with a nice string skip at the 11th and 10th frets of the fourth and second strings.

Phrygian mode guitar lick in the key of E major

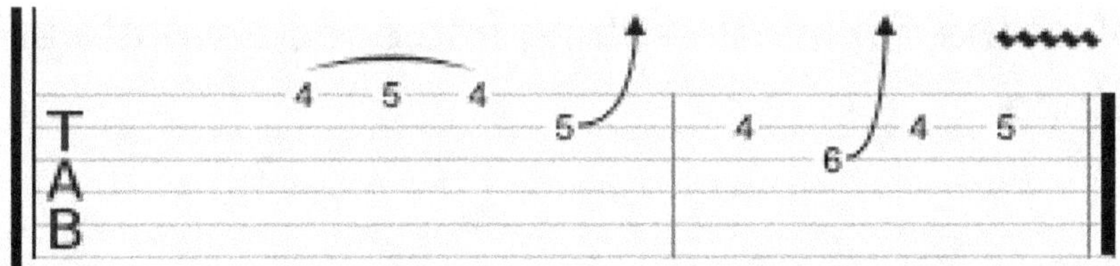

Here we have a simple hammer-on pull-off at the 4th fret first string with a couple bends at the 5th and 6th frets on the second and thirds strings. Ending with a nice vibrato at the 5th fret second string.

Lesson 35: Lydian mode guitar licks

We now come to the 4th mode, the Lydian mode. The mode that is quite different from all the rest because it is the only mode with a sharp fourth in it. Remember, this mode starts on the 4th tone degree of whatever key you choose to play it in.

Lydian mode guitar lick in the key of C major

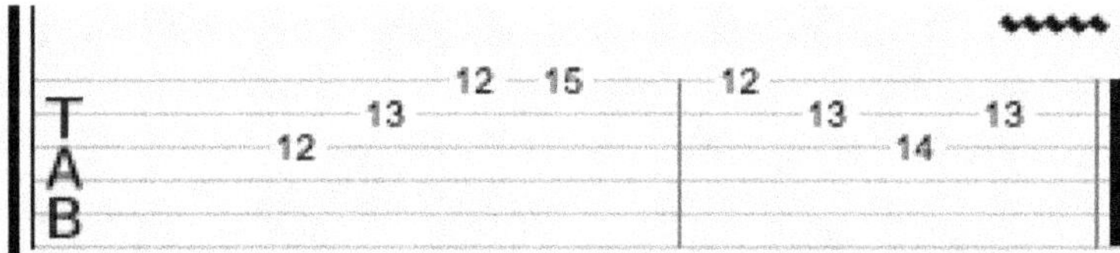

Here is a nice simple lick that goes through the mode with no frills (although you could add some) and ends with a vibrato at the 13th fret on the second string.

Lydian mode guitar lick in the key of F major

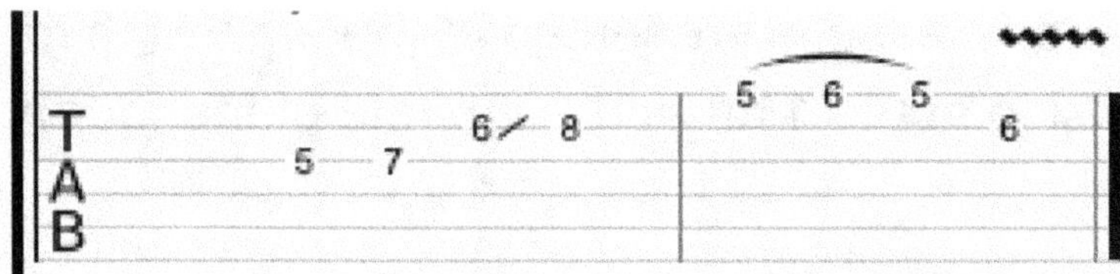

Here is a nice lick that utilizes a simple slide at the 6th fret second string as well as a hammer-on pull-off at the 5th fret first string and ends a vibrato at the 6th fret on the second string.

Lydian mode guitar lick in the key of D major

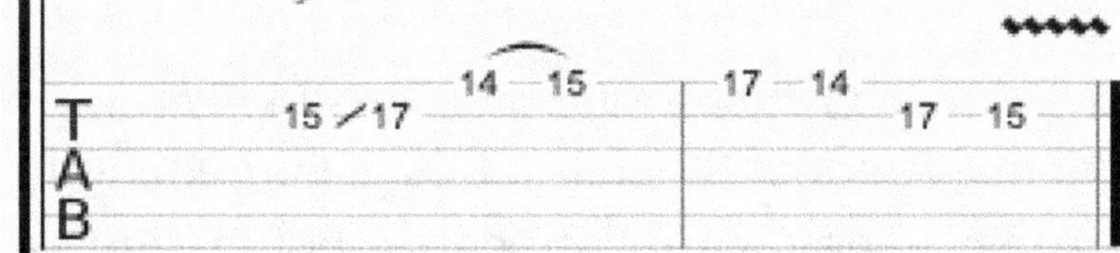

Here is a lick that starts with a slide up at the 15th fret second string and proceeds with a hammer-on at the 14th fret first string. After a few notes later it concludes with a vibrato at the 15th fret second string.

Lydian mode guitar lick in the key of G major

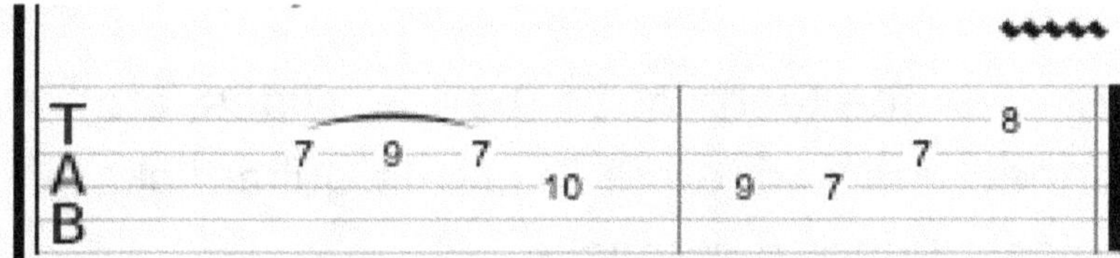

Here we have a simple hammer-on pull-off lick at the 7th fret third string with a few notes throughout the mode ending with a vibrato on the 8th fret second string.

Lydian mode guitar lick in the key of B major

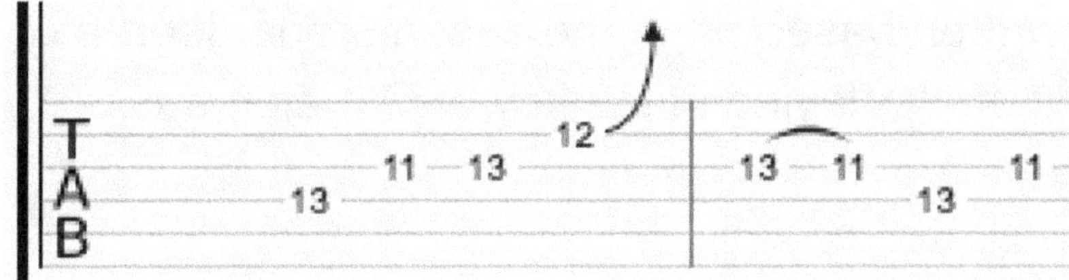

This is a nice lick that starts on the 13th fret fourth string, adds a bend at the 12th fret second string and concludes with a nice pull-off at the 13th fret third string.

Always remember to play these in the right location as they relate to the key they are being played in. If you know the mode location, you'll sound good every time because you'll be playing in key.

Chapter 7 Summary

In this chapter we have learned some very important aspects of playing guitar modes. Guitar licks. In all my years of teaching, this is something I see people miss time and time again. They learn the scales, but they miss learning the guitar licks.

Guitar licks are important to know because they are what bring the scales to life.   They make them sound like music to our ears. Make sure that you do not miss this very important aspect of playing guitar solos.

You can learn the positions and even the techniques (bends, slides, etc) but if you don't learn how to connect them together to create guitar licks, your playing will sound mechanical. Learn guitar licks.

Ionian mode guitar licks are written based off of the first tone degree in the major key. If it's in the key of C, it will be played in the ionian mode off of the C note.

Dorian mode guitar licks are written based off of the second tone degree of the major scale they come out of. If playing in the key of G major, this mode will be off of the A note.

Phrygian mode guitar licks are written based off of the third tone degree of the key it comes out of. In the key of E major, this mode will be off of the G# note.

Lydian mode guitar licks are written based off of the fourth tone degree of the key it comes out of. In the key of A major, this mode will be at the D note.

Chapter 8 Mode Licks Continued

Lesson 36: Mixolydian mode guitar licks

Now we come to the mode that is played on the 5th tone degree of the major scale. The Mixolydian mode. This mode is unique in the fact that it has all natural notes except for the flat 7. I'd call it a dominant mode for this reason.

Mixolydian mode guitar lick in C major

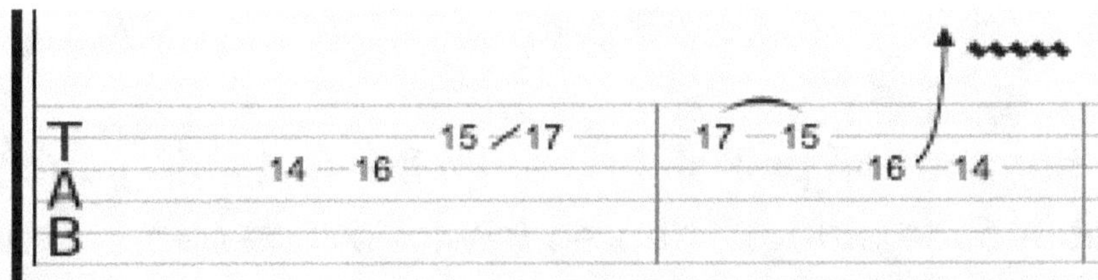

Here is a nice simple lick that utilizes a slide at the 15th fret second string followed by a pull-off at the 17th fret same string. It concludes with a bend at the 16th fret third string and a vibrato at the 14th fret third string.

Mixolydian mode guitar lick in E major

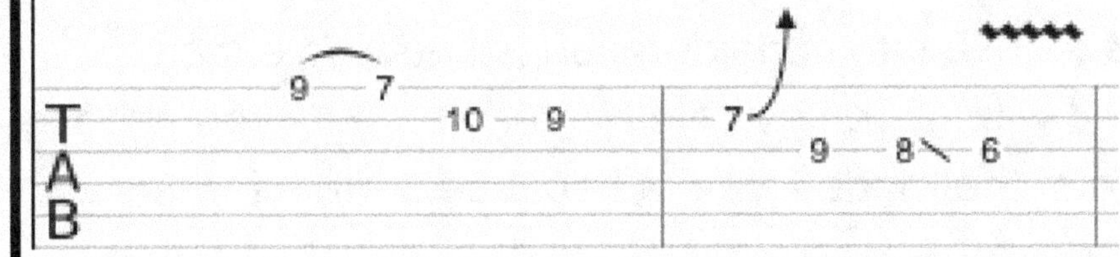

Here we start with a pull-off at the 9th fret first string and proceed through the mode. Add a bend at the 7th fret second string and end the lick with a slide down from the 8th fret third string. Followed by a vibrato at the 6th fret on the same string.

88

Mixolydian mode guitar lick in the key of F major

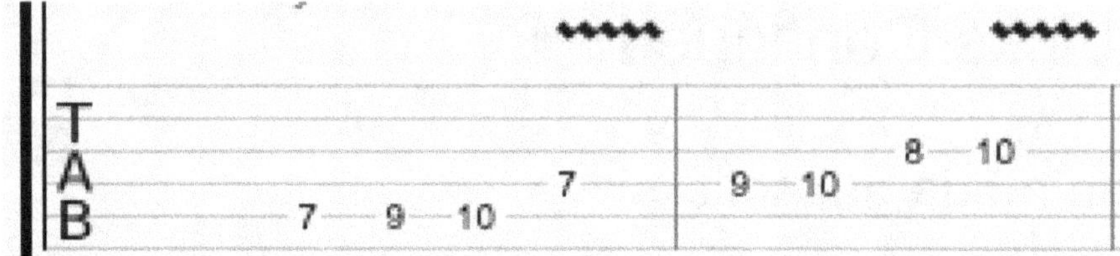

Here is a simple lick through the mode that just utilizes vibrato at the 7th fret fourth string and another vibrato at the 10th fret third string.

Mixolydian mode guitar lick in the key of D major

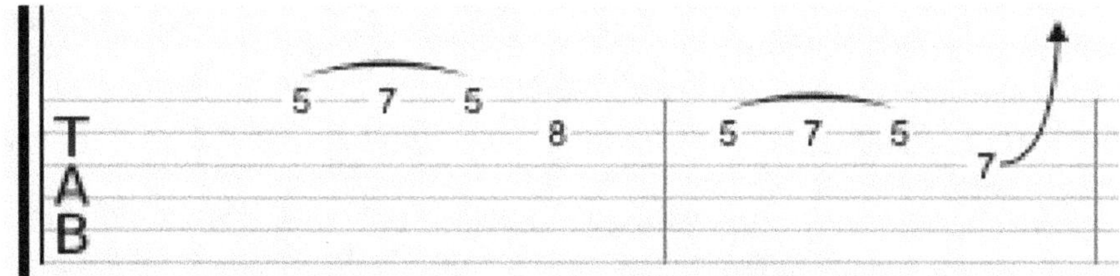

This lick starts with a nice hammer-on pull-off at the 5th fret first string and also has one at the 5th fret second string. Then ends with a nice bend up at the 7th fret third string.

Remember, that you want to make sure you can locate the mode within the key. If you're in the key of C major the mode would be played at the fifth tone degree, the G note. This can be at either the third or fifteenth fret.

The main thing you want to take into consideration is knowing exactly where the mode is located within the key. No matter what key you choose to play in. Also take note of the mode formula because certain modes will work better with certain chords.

Since the Mixolydian mode has a flat 7th in it, this tells us that it would be a great mode to play over dominant 7 chords. Chords such as G7, A7, D7, etc. Make sure you pay attention to this. It will really make a difference in which mode will sound best over certain chords.

Lesson 37: Aeolian mode guitar licks

We now come to the natural minor mode. The Aeolian mode. This mode has the flattened 3rd, 6th, & 7th. So this tells us it would work well with minor chords.

Aeolian mode guitar lick in the key of C major

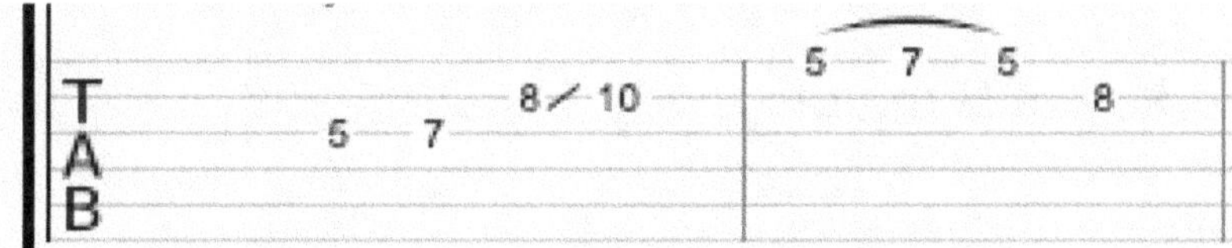

Here is a simple lick that utilizes a slide up at the 8th fret second string followed by a hammer-on pull-off at the 5th fret first string.

Aeolian mode guitar lick in the key of E major

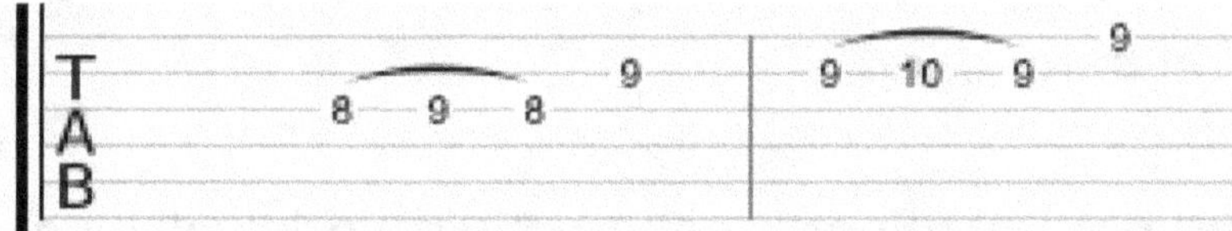

Here we start with a hammer-on pull-off at the 8th fret third string, go through the mode and execute another one at the 9th fret second string.

Aeolian mode guitar lick in the key of G major

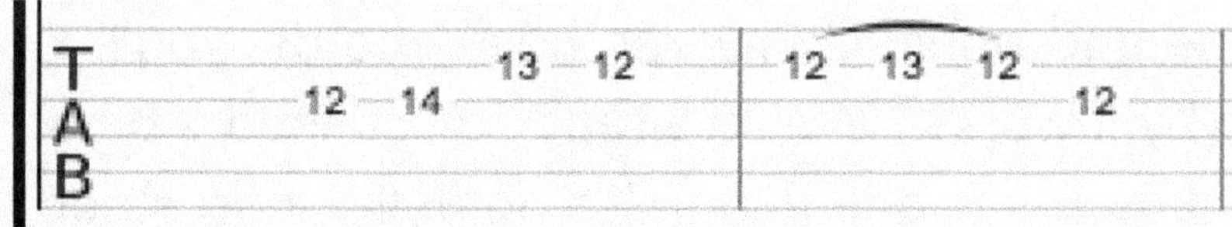

This is a nice lick that moves through the mode and executes a hammer-on pull-off at the 12th fret second string.

Remember, these are small pieces of music that can be mixed & matched in any key. These licks will teach you the art of phrasing.

90

Aeolian mode guitar lick in the key of D major

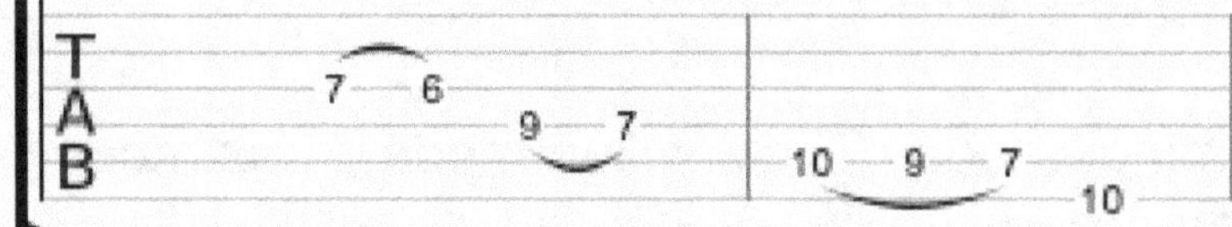

This lick is made up of all pull-offs except the last note. Starting at the 7th fret third string, proceeding through the mode at the 9th fret fourth string ending with a double pull-off at the 10th fret fifth string.

Aeolian mode guitar lick in the key of B major

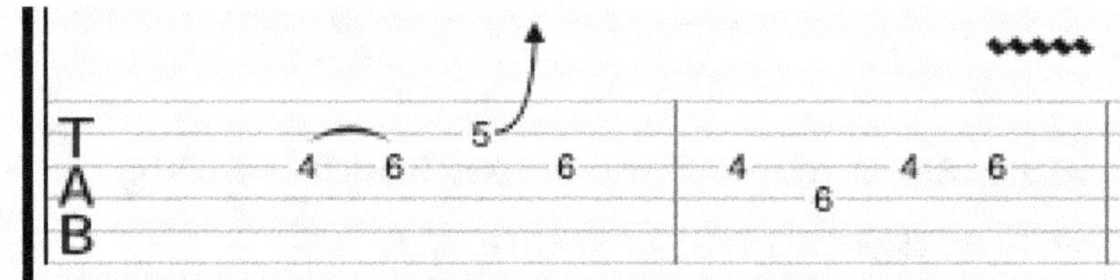

Here we start with a hammer-on at the 4th fret third string and bend up at the 5th fret second string. We then proceed through the mode and end the lick with a vibrato at the 6th fret third string.

Also remember, that this is the natural minor mode and will work well with any of the chords we previously learned that come out of it. All the guitar modes will work with this phylosophy. That's why it is important to know the scale mode formula by memory.

The more you know this mode and work with it over these chords, you'll begin to hear how and see why it works. We've already discussed a bit of why already, but knowing it in theory is one thing. It's not fully understood until you put it into practical application.

Lesson 38: Locrian mode guitar licks

We now come to the final mode. The one that is quite different from all the rest. It is the Locrian mode. The diminished mode. Do you remember why it is called the diminished mode?

It is because it has both the flat 3rd, & 5th notes in it. Whenever you take a major triad (1 3 5) and flatten both the 3rd and 5th (1 b3 b5) you get a diminished chord. Same goes for the Locrian mode.

Here we have a mode that has the flat 2nd, 3rd, 5th, 6th, & 7th. You can clearly see why it is a diminished mode. By knowing this we can choose when to use it best. Minor chords, diminished chords, etc.

Let's look at some guitar licks within this mode

Locrian mode guitar licks in the key of C major

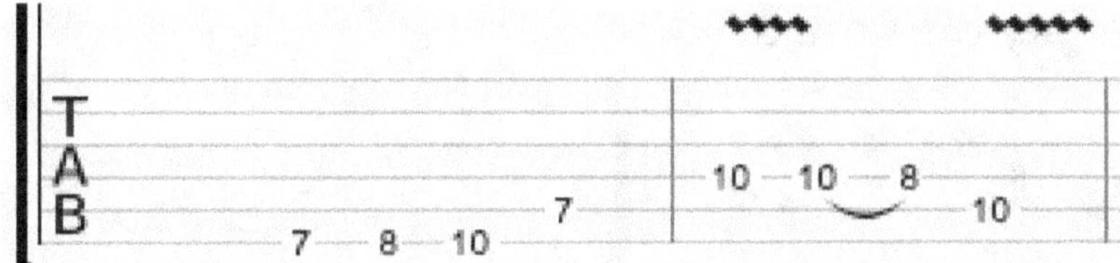

Hre we have a simple lick that starts with the seventh note on the sixth string, proceeds through the mode and stops with a vibrato at the 10th fret fourth string. Then starts up again with a pull-off at the 10th fret fourth string and ends again with a vibrato at the 10th fret fifth string,

Locrian mode guitar lick in the key of F major

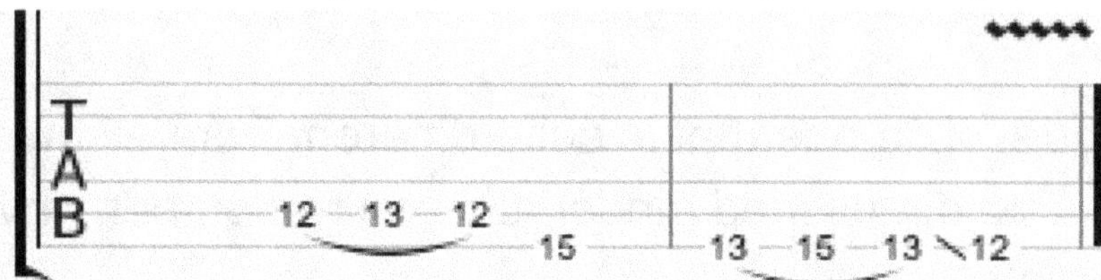

Here is a simple lick utilizing a hammer-on pull-off at the 12th fret fifth string and at the 13th fret of the 6th string sliding down to the 12th fret and ending with a vibrato.

Locrian mode guitar lick in the key of D major

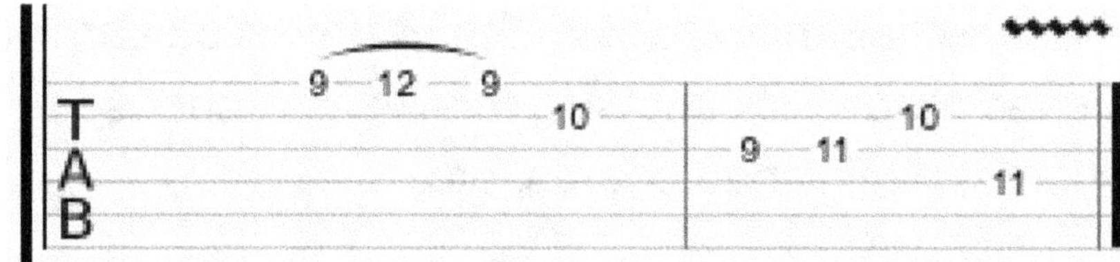

Here we start with a hammer-on pull-off at the 9th fret first string, proceed through the mode and end with vibrato on the 11th fret fourth string.

Locrian mode guitar lick in the key of A major

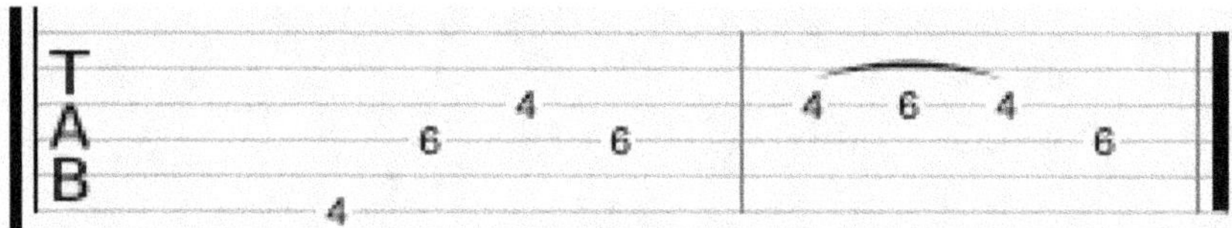

Here is a nice lick that starts with an octave at the 4th fret sixth string. Skips the fifth proceeds through the mode and adds a hammer-on pull-off at the 4th fret third string and ends at the 6th fret fourth string.

Remember, this mode is exactly the same as the Ionian mode except for the one note difference. But it is this one note difference that gives the mode its character.

Lesson 39: Arpeggiating the modes

One of the cool things that you can do with plenty of practice is arpeggiating the modes. This is where you play across the mode in an ascending and descending manner. This gives you a different type of sound and allows you to execute different techniques.

For this example we will use the key of G major. This will give us plenty of room to go through the modes along the fretboard. So like the other examples, one will be given in each mode.

Arpeggio in the G Ionian mode

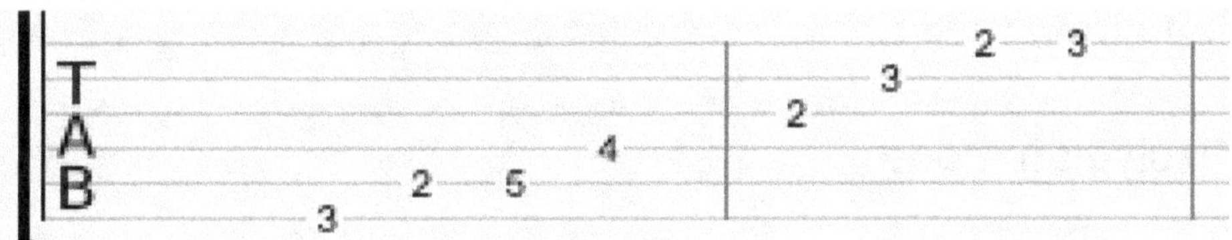

Here we start on the G note sixth string, progress through the mode and end on the G note first string.

Arpeggio in the A Dorian mode

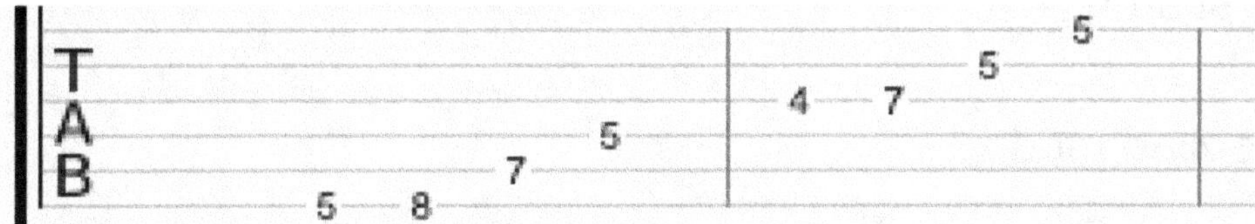

Here we start on the A note sixth string, progress through the mode and end on the A note first string.

Arpeggio in the B Phrygian mode

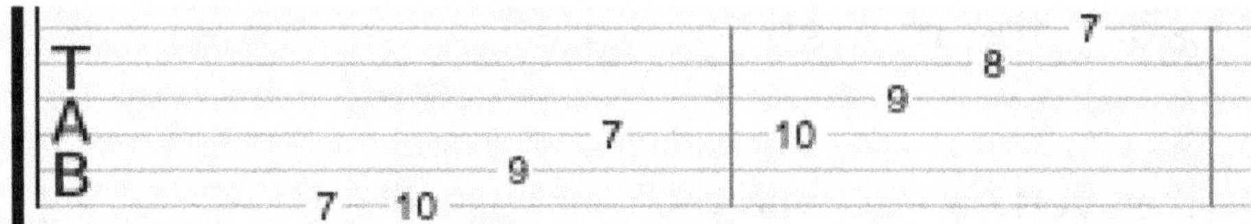

Here we start on the B note sixth string, proceed through the mode and end on the B note first string.

Arpeggio in the C Lydian mode

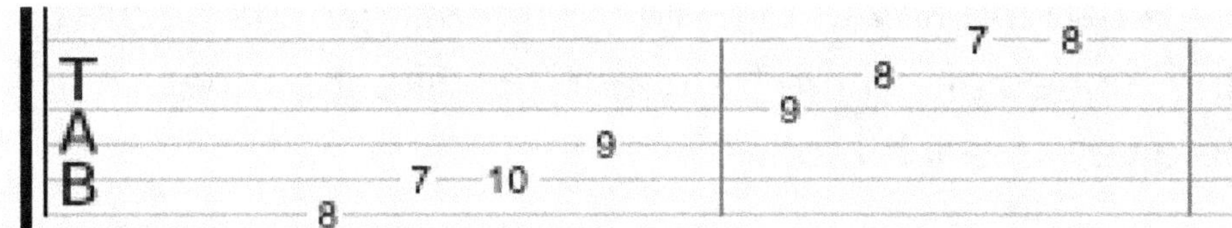

Here we start on the C note 6th string, proceed through the mode and end on the C note first string.

Arpeggio in the D Mixolydian mode

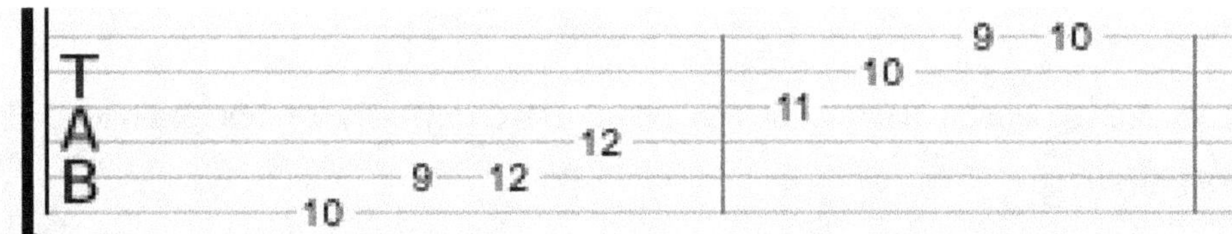

Here we start on the D note sixth string, proceed through the mode and end on the D note first string.

Arpeggio in the E Aeolian mode

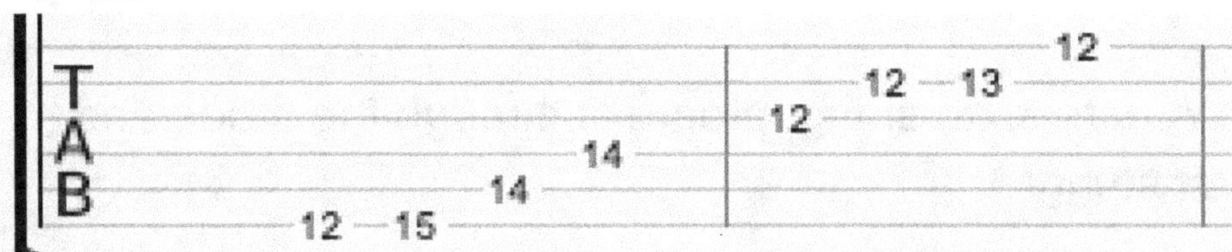

Here we start on the E note sixth string, proceed through the mode and end on the E note first string.

Arpeggio in the F# Locrian mode

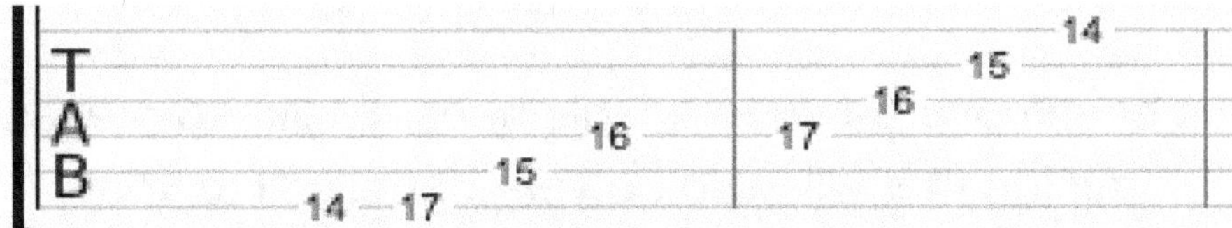

Here we start on the F# note sixth string, proceed through the mode and end on the F# note first string.

We have created an arpeggio in each of the 7 modes in the key of G. Notice how there are no hammer-ons, bends or anything like that. These are just single notes run through the mode. Usually chords played individually.

Since there are many chords that can be created in each mode as we learned earlier, there are multiple arpeggios that can be created. You just have to find the chord within the mode and play the notes individually.

Arpeggios give you a good understanding of the modes, chords, & notes along the fretboard. I highly recommend you don't overlook them as they can be a huge benefit not only to your understanding of music, but to the kinds of sounds you can make with your guitar playing.

Lesson 40: Additional guitar training

In addition to all that has been covered so far in this book, I'd like to present you with some additional training that will also be very beneficial to your learning. Not just in learning modes, but in aspects of your guitar playing.

Practice Habits

One thing that will make all the difference in your guitar playing and understanding of the music language is your practice habits. I highly recommend you develop some.

Design a good <u>practice place</u>. Bedroom, basement, garage, etc. A studio that you can focus on your studies.

Commit to a dedicated <u>practice time</u>. This tells the mind it's time to study and practice. It allows you to focus on guitar and only guitar.

Develop a <u>practice routine</u>. Decide what it is you need to work on and break it down into sections. 10 min warm-up, 10 min chords review, 10 min strumming, 10 min music theory, 10 min scales, 10 min improv, etc.

Remember, learning music is an engagement of mental, physical, and spiritual faculties. And the way you choose to practice and study on a daily basis will make a huge difference on their development.

Ear Training

This is an element of playing guitar that you always want to be working on. Developing the ability to hear note intervals. This will help in recognizing chords and the modes they come out of. Here are a few exercises to help develop this ability.

1. <u>Go through scales</u> in each key slowly and really listen for the notes. By doing this your ear will get familiar with the pitch of notes along the fretboard.

2. <u>Play one note</u> and try to hum or sound out the next one in the scale. By doing this you get the ear and whole body to resonate with the pitch of the note.

3. <u>Hum simple melodies</u> that contain a few notes and try to duplicate. Then play the song, review your results and see how close you become at getting it correct.

4. <u>Play the first note of a scale</u> and hum or sing the rest of the notes. Then play the notes on your guitar and see how close you come to being correct.

Ear Training takes time. It is the development of becoming one with the guitar. That is why many guitar players can play by ear and get results. It comes from hours and hours of having that guitar in hand and practicing.

98

Improvisation

Another key element of guitar playing is being able to improvise. No matter if you play rhythm or solos, improvisation is a must to master. And this also only develops through time.

Time of study and practice. Practicing your chords, progressions, and scales. It is the art of being able to make stuff up on the spot.

There are usually two ways that guitar players create and record.

1. <u>Methodical phrasing</u>.
They sit down and methodically create ideas and then record them.

2. <u>Spontaneous combustion</u>.
They create on the spot (improvise) and record the moment.

Both ways are very beneficial. For our purposes here, we will focus on the latter. Improvising. Creating on the spot. This is a skill that you want to focus on developing.

Very much like a comedian who just makes stuff up on the spot, that is what you want to be able to do. If you take all the previous lessons taught so far and put them into action, you will be able to do this.

But it takes time. Just like ear training. You must put in the time and do the work to see the results. As a guitar player specializing in melody, you might need to do this if you choose to play with someone. They throw out a key and expect you to come up with something that sounds good.

With the information you have learned in this training guide you should have absolutely no problem doing so. That is provided that you've done your homework.

Remember, you don't want to just read the book and know it in theory. You want to put the lessons into practice! Theory is one thing, but practical application is where you are going to see the best results.

Here are a few tips to help you with improvising.

1. Know all your notes on all six strings along the fretboard.
This is one thing that cannot be stressed enough. I can't begin to tell you how many guitar players do not know this. Especially ones who play by ear.

Playing by ear is fine. As I mentioned the importance of ear training, but make sure you know your notes on all six strings. The faster you can pick them out, the quicker you'll be able to find chords, create new chords, and the same goes for scales.

2. Know exactly where all 12 keys are located. This can be done by knowing the notes on the 6th string.

This kind of goes with the previous step. But more so because if you know where all twelve keys are on the fretboard and you're in a situation that calls for you to play a solo in the key of D minor, you'll know where that's at and be able to compose something in the correct position fairly quickly.

This will also help you with knowing where each mode is as well in any particular key. Especially if you know what mode goes well over what type of chords.

3. Know all 7 modes (and any other scales you've learned) well enough to be able to "visualize" them on the fretboard. See how they connect to one another and span the entire fretboard.

This is vitally important as it will allow you to find where you need to be quickly. You'll be able to decide what mode you want to play in and what guitar licks or arpeggios might sound best.

If you know exactly where they are on the fretboard and how they connect, you can play anywhere! In the lower position for part of the progression, then possibly move further up the neck for other parts of the song. Knowing your positioning will make a huge difference.

4. Know how to properly execute all the guitar licks, arpeggios and techniques associated with them.

This is a huge must. That is why I presented this information in this training guide. It gives you examples to follow. Do this enough and you'll be able to come up with your own guitar licks and arpeggios. Remember, that's what melody lines and guitar solos are made up of. Guitar licks.

Knowing how to execute them and create new ones is what turns the modes and any other scales (like the pentatonics) into music. But in order to do so, you must master the techniques. The hammer-ons, pull-offs, bends, slides, vibrato, etc.

5. Know how to create chords and chord progressions so you can play melodies over the top of them and sound good every time.

This is why we went over this earlier in the training. You didn't overlook it did you? I hope not. If so, go back over it because this is where it is really going to benefit you.

By knowing how to create majors, minors, etc, chords, you'll be able to create any type of emotion you choose. And by being able to put them together to create chord progressions you'll be able to sound like a world class musician.

Like I stated before, by knowing what chords come out of each mode and being able to play melody over the top of them, you are going to sound great every time! Why? Because the chords and modes directly relate to each other.

6. Practice, practice, practice, and practice some more!

Of course this goes without saying, but will be mentioned anyway for good measure. You must put this information into practice! As I said before, it's one thing to know this in theory (a lot of people who study theory do) but it's something else to be able to put it into practical application.

Most guitar players I know who study theory and only theory are great with theory. But since they don't write or play songs, they don't practice the application part of it.

Oh, they're great at writing the chord charts and telling me what chords are in each key, but if I ask them to put all that theory into song, they don't do so well. That's because they are missing the "application" part of it. You must apply what you are learning.

When guitar players play by ear, they practice the application part of it. But they don't study the theory part. That's why if you ask them what they are playing, most of the time they don't know. At least not the technical terms or why the notes work together. They just know they do.

You want to be better than that. You don't need to know everything under the sun about the guitar or even music in general, but you do want to know what you are playing and be able to explain why it works.

If you apply all these ideas on a daily basis, I guarantee that you will become great at improvising. But like I said before, it does and will not come overnight. It takes time to master. Put in the work, see the results. It's that simple.

Chapter 8 Summary

In this chapter we have learned some excellent points when it comes to learning modes. First we continue the mode guitar licks, then move to arpeggios and additional training.

<u>Mixolydian mode guitar licks</u> are written based off of the 5th tone degree of the major scale they come out of. Remember, this mode has the b7 and works well with dominant chords. In the key of G, this mode will be off of the D note.

<u>Aeolian mode guitar licks</u> are written off of the sixth tone degree of the major scale they come out of. Remember, this is the natural minor mode and worlds well with minor chords. In the key of C, this would be off of the A note.

<u>Locrian mode guitar licks</u> are written off of the seventh tone degree of the major scale they come out of. Remember, this is the diminished mode and works well with diminished chords. In the key of F, this would be off of the E note.

<u>Arpeggiating the modes</u> is also a good way of playing them. This is where you play chord notes within the modes individually. Here you just play the notes. No bends, slides, etc. Just play the chord notes individually to create a unique sound.

Arpeggios are a great way to create a fast flowing sound and can add a "kick to your improvisational skills. Because they contain the notes of a chord, you can use them to link what's going on in the chord structure beneath your solo.

This kind of technical phrasing will benefit your overall ability to play and understand music in multiple ways. But the main thing it will do is create muscle memory. And it is this muscle memory that will help you to become a great musician.

Remember, these arpeggios can be done with any chord in any mode.

<u>Additional guitar training</u> is provided to push you into excellence even further. Practice habits, ear training, and improvising. These techniques are all very important for all aspects of your guitar playing. So don't overlook them.

The better practice habits you create, the better off you will be. It's that simple. Make sure to really study this part of the training. It will determine if you become a good guitar player, or a great guitar player.

Ear training will develop over time with practice. The more you have the guitar in your hand the better it will be. And if you go through the training exercises I have presented, you'll see this ability develop.

Improvising is the best skill of all because it allows you to be creative and have fun. I recommend you practice discipline first by getting down the guitar licks and chords I have shown you. Once you have those fully understood and can execute them properly, then you'll be ready.

Mastering The Modes Quiz

I think it is very important for you to test yourself to see if you fully understand the lessons in this training guide.

It is always a good idea to see what has stuck to memory and what hasn't. Music is a language and just like any other language, there are many aspects to its learning and development.

I hold no doubt that some of the lessons will come easy to you, and some of them will have you scratching your head. This is understandable. Anytime we learn new information, our minds tend to do this. I can't mention how many times this has happened to me.

But don't worry. If something isn't making sense as quickly as you'd like it to, just take a break and come back to it. You'll see that it will and the light bulb will go on over your head.

I have presented the material in the simplest format possible in order for it to be easily understandable, so you shouldn't have too many issues. Just take your time with it and let time develop your mental and physical faculties.

With all that being said, let's take a look at the test. It will not be too hard. Just a question from each of the lessons. The answers can be found in each one. If you don't know something, just go back to the lesson and review. You'll get it.

Write your answers here or on a separate sheet of paper. Remember, reading and writing go hand in hand, so don't overlook this.

Q: What is a mode?
A: ____

Q: Is a mode the same as a scale?
A: ____

Q: Why learn to use modes?
A: ____

Q: What kind of notation is most common for guitar?
A: ____

Q: What are mode diagrams?
A: ____

Q: What notes are in the C major scale?
A: ____

Q: What notes are in the G major scale?
A: ____

Q: What notes are in the D major scale?
A: ____

Q: What notes are in the A major scale?
A: ____

Q: What notes are in the E major scale?

A: ____

Q: Is the Ionian mode, major or minor?

A: ____

Q: Is the Dorian mode major or minor?

A: ____

Q: Is the Phrygian mode major or minor?

A: ____

Q: Is the Lydian mode major or minor?

A: ____

Q: Is the Mixolydian mode major or minor?

A: ____

Q: Is the Aeolian mode major or minor?

A: ____

Q: Is the Locrian mode major or minor?

A: ____

Q: What does natural minor mean?

A: ____

Q: How do whole steps and half steps relate to scales?

A: ____

Q: Why can you bring the modes down to only 5?
A: _______________________________________

Q: What is the Ionian mode scale formula?
A: _______________________________________

Q: What is the Dorian mode scale formula?
A: _______________________________________

Q: What is the Phrygian mode scale formula?
A: _______________________________________

Q: What is the Lydian mode scale formula?
A: _______________________________________

Q: What is the Mixolydian mode scale formula?
A: _______________________________________

Q: What is the Aeolian mode scale formula?
A: _______________________________________

Q: What is the locrian mode scale formula?
A: _______________________________________

Q: What are mode chords?
A: _______________________________________

Q: What is a chord progression?
A: _______________________________________

Q: Why learn finger dexterity exercises?

A: ___________________________________

Q: Why are guitar licks important?

A: ___________________________________

Q: What is a hammer-on?

A: ___________________________________

Q: What is a pull-off?

A: ___________________________________

Q: What is a hammer-on pull-off?

A: ___________________________________

Q: What is a bend?

A: ___________________________________

Q: What is a slide?

A: ___________________________________

Q: What is trill?

A: ___________________________________

Q: What is vibrato?

A: ___________________________________

Q: What are arpeggios?

A: ___________________________________

Q: Why are they important?

A: ____

Q: Why develop good practice habits?

A: ____

Q: What exercise example is good for ear training?

A; ____

Q: What is the importance of improvisation?

A: ____

How well did you do? This quiz is for you and you only so no worries if you missed some things. There is a lot here to digest so if you need to go back and review some lessons, feel free to do so.

Remember, there are many <u>benefits </u>to taking a test like this and it is why this quiz is presented in the training.

1. It aids in later retention of the information that you have studied and practiced. Later retention is a must when it comes to learning something new. Especially when it comes to putting it into practical application.

2. It helps you to identify gaps in the knowledge that you have learned. Many times when we learn something new our mind doesn't quite get it all.

There are things that we need to go over a second and possibly a third time to fully comprehend. And that's ok. As long as we know this and are willing to do so, taking a test can help with this.

3. It helps you to produce a better organization of the knowledge that you have learned. It helps you to categorize information and put it into different parts of the memory bank for future retrieval.

4. It improves your transfer of new knowledge into concepts and techniques. This is very important when it comes to learning music, because it is all about concepts and techniques.

5. Taking a simple quiz like this helps with all these things. It is very important that you fully comprehend all the techniques, concepts, and theory that goes into the modes to get the most out of them.

"If you did good on all the questions, then congratulations on all your efforts. You now have an excellent understanding of modes and how they work."

Guitar Modes Final Conclusion

If you've gone all the way through the book and gotten this far, I congratulate you on your retention and persistence. I'd like to also say "thank you for your time and purchase of this book" as you seem like the kind of student I'd like to teach in person.

In this training guide you have learned many things about the modes. What they are, how to find them, when to use them, and why they are a good idea to learn.

Although this training guide does not teach you everything there is to learn about modes (if it did, it would be the size of an encyclopedia) it does teach you the fundamental principles and concepts that are needed to build a solid foundation.

I can't begin to tell you how many guitar students and guitar players I meet that skip over the fundamentals. I guess because they felt they were boring to learn. The problem with this approach is that they run into roadblocks and hurdles they can't get over.

That is when they seek out someone like me.

After talking with them for a few minutes, I can see very clearly where their problem is. Lack of fundamental knowledge and application. I recommend you do not become one of these guitar players. If you take the time to focus and fully understand the fundamentals of the game, you'll develop potential for greatness.

Because the truth of the matter is, that mastery in any subject stands on the shoulders of the fundamentals. That is why a lot of my books are written in this area. It is the most important to master.

Learn and remember the 7 modes. Where they are in each key. Master which ones are major and which ones are minor. Also remember the Locrian mode is diminished.

Master what chords can be played out of each mode. Develop the ability to put these chords together in a chord progression so that you can play the modes over the top of them.

Master guitar licks and arpeggios to solo with style. Be able to do this over the chords and progressions that you create. Master the techniques needed to bring the modes to life.

Focus on training your ear and master the art of improvising. That way if someone says "I got a song in G and need a solo over the top" you'll be able to say "no problem" with confidence.

Master developing great practice habits and become an inspiration for others to look up to.

Master the fundamentals, build a solid foundation, and you'll be able to accomplish anything. I guarantee it.

Best of luck and most of all, have fun!

Sincerely, Dwayne Jenkins
Tritone Publishing. Copyright © 202

Other Books That Can Help You

In addition to this book, I have authored other books that can help improve your guitar playing. If you need help with rhythm I recommend you check out the book:

Rhythm Guitar Alchemy

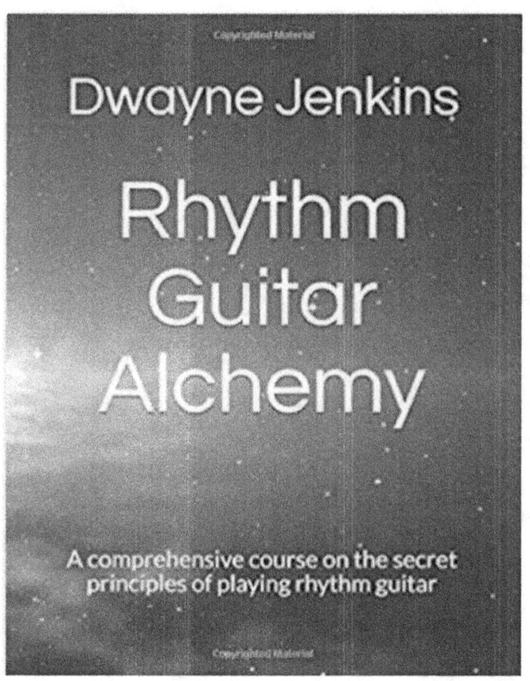

A simple step-by-step method book based on the science of playing rhythm guitar. It will teach you chord theory, strumming & arpeggiating chords. Along with developing your timing to enhance your rhythm playing. Rhythm Guitar Alchemy is a great addition to Learn To Play Guitar Modes.

In addition to that book, I think you can benefit from my other book I've authored and published on playing guitar solos:

Lead Guitar Wizardry

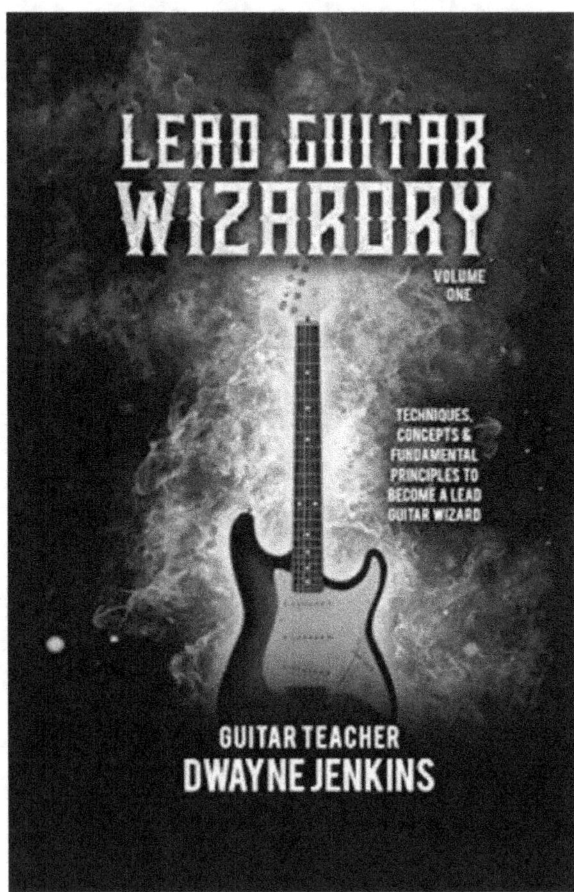

This book introduces you to the pentatonic scales and how they can really benefit your guitar playing. Not only with guitar solos, but also with your enhancement of fretboard knowledge.

This book goes over the major and minor pentatonic scales, along with the blues scale, guitar riffs, triplets, transposing, alternate picking, harmony notes, octaves, hybrid picking, sweep picking, and chord progressions to solo over.

It also teaches you about finger tapping, playing solos from recordings, and much, much more. This book is packed with knowledge to get you playing guitar solos in the right way. Anytime, everytime.

Even if you know some about playing guitar solos with the pentatonic scales, I'm sure there is something here in this training guide that can help improve your guitar playing.

So if you need any help in the area of rhythm or lead guitar playing, these two books will do the job. There is so much information presented that you'll discover something new you didn't know already.

And sometimes, it is just one new thing that can set you off into a whole new way of thinking and inspire your guitar playing.

Rhythm Guitar Alchemy is designed to teach you the science of how to improve your rhythm playing and chord construction.

Lead Guitar Wizardry is designed to get you on the path to playing jaw dropping guitar solos that'll make people go "wow!"

Not only will you be able to do these things, but you'll develop a full comprehensive understanding of why they work the way they do.

Most guitar players don't have that.

About The Author

Dwayne Jenkins is a professional private guitar teacher and accomplished musician who has been learning, playing, and teaching guitar lessons throughout Denver, CO for almost two decades.

He is now bringing his special training methods and practices that have been honed and hand crafted throughout the years on how to play guitar to students around the world.

Dwayne has a unique and exciting approach that gets students of all ages and skill levels enjoying the fun of playing guitar. His enthusiasm and love for teaching shine through with every lesson he creates.

His lessons are designed to enhance your ability to progress. No matter your reason for learning guitar, there will always be something in Dwayne's guitar books and products to help you achieve your dreams.

So if you're a student looking to start, or a student looking to further your education, be sure to get involved with Dwayne's guitar lessons.

What students are saying about Dwayne's Guitar Books & Lessons

Dwayne's Books offer a lot of great information.   His lessons are great for learning and very helpful. He covers a lot of stuff. From chords, scales,riffs, structure of practicing and much more. BUY ALL HIS BOOKS! And read them. Then, pick up your guitar and use what's in the books. If you study them, you will notice a big difference after a couple weeks. Learn from the books, practice, practice, practice, and you'll see it's well worth it. Thank you. **James**

I bought your "How To Play Guitar Solos" book, absolutely phenomenal so far. Was in a rut with my playing recently as I could play decent rhythm but struggled with soloing. Good job man. **Euan**

Dwayne, your topics are very helpful, I appreciate the instructional teachings! I hope more people will be exposed to your educational wealth! Thanks again to Colorado's best guitar teacher Dwayne! **Flame Symmetry**

Dwayne's books are well written and easy to follow. I would definitely recommend his books to anyone wanting to learn guitar. You can easily find them on Amazon. **Betty**

My daughter has been playing with Dwayne for 6 months. Not only does she love her guitar, but he is such a great teacher. His methods work! I highly recommend his books if you can't get him in person. **Elina**

The book Learn To Play Acoustic Guitar is a sure path to learning how to play an acoustic guitar! It will provide a pleasant learning experience as it covers everything a beginner needs to know. This book is straightforward and it's really nice to be able to practice as you read through the lessons, not just read. There are plenty of examples and diagrams to help the reader better understand how to play. I also really appreciated that you're given recommendations on what type/brand of equipment is worth looking into for things like guitar picks or a tuner. Lastly I'd like to acknowledge that you're also provided access for personal help, after all, nothing beats an actual teacher! All in all, this is an excellent book to get you started on playing acoustic. **Michelle**

At the age of 60, I decided to try to learn to play guitar. I'm a singer and want to be able to accompany myself instead of always relying on finding an instrumentalist. Several years ago I tried taking lessons from a friend but didn't feel I was making any progress and gave up after a short time. My friend was a good guitarist but he wasn't a teacher. What a difference it has made taking lessons with Dwayne! Not only is he a very nice guy, but he is also great at checking in to see how I'm doing and is totally approachable. In only a few weeks I'm playing, singing some 3 – 5 chord songs. Dwayne assigns clear and concise "homework" with a variety of techniques which makes it interesting and fun to practice. I highly recommend him as a guitar teacher. **Madelaine**

I have taken lessons from many guitar teachers throughout the years and none of them have allowed me to progress in such a short time or have made learning as fun as Dwayne Jenkins. I now feel that I am actually getting somewhere with the instrument. I have learned more in two months with Dwayne than I had in two years with other teachers. Do you want to get better? Do you want to have fun learning the guitar? Then pick Dwayne, I guarantee you'll see positive results quickly! **John**